CHURCH MATTERS

God's original purpose for
the church and why it matters

© 2018 by TGS International, a wholly owned subsidiary of Christian Aid Ministries, Berlin, Ohio.

All rights reserved. No part of this book may be used, reproduced, or stored in any retrieval system, in any form or by any means, electronic or mechanical, without written permission from the publisher except for brief quotations embodied in critical articles and reviews.

ISBN: 978-1-947319-39-4

Illustrations: Igor Kondratyuk

Cover and text layout design: Kristi Yoder

Printed in the USA

Second printing: September 2018

Published by:
TGS International
P.O. Box 355
Berlin, Ohio 44610 USA
Phone: 330.893.4828
Fax: 330.893.2305
www.tgsinternational.com

TGS001771

GARY MILLER

CHURCH MATTERS

Where there is no vision,
the people perish.
Proverbs 29:18

Table of Contents

Part One: The Purpose of Church 7
   1. Modern Evangelical Christianity 9
   2. Are We on the Right Track? 17
   3. The Vibrant Church: A Coordinated Contradiction 23
   4. Church: What Did God Have in Mind? 31
   5. What Kind of Music Is Your Church Producing? 37

Part Two: Church and Culture 47
   6. When the Symphony Goes Sour 49
   7. The Challenge of Culture 55
   8. Culture: Examining Our Relationship 63
   9. Culture: How Much Should We Embrace? 71
  10. Finding Moderation Without Compromise 81

Part Three: Business and Brotherhood:
             Rethinking the Relationship 87
  11. Business and Brotherhood: The Problem 89
  12. Is Business a Blessing? 97
  13. Business: Understanding the Potential 103
  14. Connecting Vocations with Vision 109

Part Four: Are We Limiting God? 117
    15. Limiting God 119
    16. Current Challenges 125
    17. Current "Christian" Cultural Challenges 133
    18. "So Send I You" 141
    19. Programmed Evangelism 149

Part Five: The Power and Purpose of Oneness 157
    20. Last Words: Famous or Forgotten? 159
    21. The Devastation of Divorce 169
    22. Grounds for Divorce? 177

Part Six: What Is God's Vision? 185
    23. How Big Is Your Vision? 187
    24. Strong versus Weak Churches 195
    25. The Christian Community Commitment 203
    26. Honesty About Who We Are 215
    27. A Path Forward 223

Endnotes 233
About the Author 237
Additional Resources by Gary Miller 239

PART ONE

The
PURPOSE
of Church

CHAPTER ONE

Modern Evangelical Christianity

In the late 1940s, just after World War II, manufacturers of margarine in the United States had a problem. Their product was good, but sales were poor. Since the arrival of imitation butter from France in the 1870s, outraged American dairy farmers had protested its promotion. Pressure was placed on legislators, and laws were enacted which made its sale difficult in some states and illegal in others.

Margarine, its enemies said, was a direct threat to the family farm and the American way of life. Lobbyists funded anti-margarine activists, who spread cartoons of factories producing margarine in huge vats and dropping in stray cats, arsenic, and rubber boots. Some spread rumors that the mix of chemicals in margarine caused cancer. Others said eating it could lead to insanity. By 1902, over half the states in America had enacted laws requiring the product to be a color other than yellow. A few even demanded that it be dyed pink in order to be sold in their state.[1] However, over time these laws were repealed, the fears behind them faded, and margarine was allowed on grocery store shelves.

The product now tasted almost like butter, looked like butter, was cheaper than butter, and was said to be healthier than butter. But it still did not sell. In desperation, manufacturers turned to a man with an uncanny ability to market hard-to-sell products.

Louis Cheskin had spent his life observing people and determining why they purchased the products they did. He investigated how packaging affected people's perception of value and quality. One of Cheskin's most notable discoveries was that people are apparently unable to resist transferring their feelings about the packaging to the product itself. He did many studies in which he asked participants to compare several products, the only variable being the box or wrapper. He discovered that consumers gave entirely different answers about taste and quality when the packaging was changed.

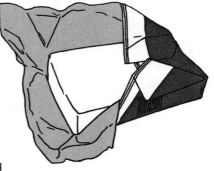

Cheskin took Marlboro cigarettes, originally designed for women and selling poorly, repackaged and advertised them using a rugged Western theme,[2] and sales began to climb. He accomplished similar turnarounds for Betty Crocker products and Tide soap. What could he do with margarine?

Through numerous studies, Cheskin determined that perception was the problem, not taste; people still saw margarine as an inferior product. So he told the manufacturer to make two simple alterations: change the wrapper and give it a more sophisticated name. So they wrapped the margarine in foil, a symbol of quality at the time, and changed the name to Imperial.[3] The results were astounding! Within a few years, margarine was a strong contender in America as a spread for bread.

A little creativity in marketing can achieve astonishing things. Louis Cheskin was a master at finding consumers' core longings and convincing them that the product he was marketing would fulfill their desires. He understood the power of repackaging products that are difficult to sell.

Selling Christianity

If there were a list of things whose attributes render them difficult to market, the original Gospel of Jesus Christ would have to be near the top. Imagine trying to sell something that promises to cause conflict in your family,[a] appears foolish to your peers,[b] garners hate from society,[c] and guarantees suffering and persecution to those who pursue it.[d] How would you like to market a product like that? Yet the early apostles went into a heathen world promising this very thing. All but one of them experienced exactly what had been promised—persecution, torture, and a martyr's death. This was the message of Jesus and the early church.

The world doesn't like this kind of message. It appeared foolish to many when first presented by the apostles, and it is no more favored now. Jesus' self-denying message will never be popular with a self-absorbed public. How then have evangelists been able to attract people and expand their churches? The answer is both simple and sobering: they have repackaged Christianity. In fact, in their eagerness to pursue potential converts, many modern churches have marketed Christianity using methods straight from the playbook of Louis Cheskin: find the consumers' deepest longings, then package your product in a way that persuades them it will fulfill their desires.

> Jesus' self-denying message will never be popular with a self-absorbed public.

---

[a] Matthew 10:36
[b] 1 Corinthians 1:18
[c] Mark 13:13, Luke 21:17, John 15:18
[d] 2 Timothy 3:12

Attractive Packaging

As you consider Western society, what would you say the general public longs for? One of your first observations will be the fervent pursuit of entertainment. Boredom is not an option. People go to great lengths to find distractions and keep themselves amused. Whether following sports teams, purchasing the newest music, or discussing the latest movie, Americans are passionate about entertainment. Consequently, many churches have incorporated entertainment into their marketing strategy. Good music, expensive stage lighting, funny stories, youth programs, and audio-visual performances are designed to satisfy the seeker's thirst for fun. It isn't easy to compete with Hollywood, but churches are doing their best.

Financial wealth is another obvious craving. Once again, churches are so focused on this topic that they have wrapped "Christianity" in a package that has become known as the health and wealth gospel. Other seekers are pursuing better relationships with friends, family, and spouses. In response, pastors and writers focus their sermons, books, and seminars on the feelings and needs of the people they are trying to attract. Some churches even focus on particular themes. Are you attracted to the Wild West? You can find a church for cowboy culture that speaks of heaven as "that great roundup in the sky." Christianity is being served up any way you like it. As a seeker, you are in the driver's seat, and like the Burger King advertisement, you can "have it your way!" The church is straying from the Gospel to provide a product that pleases. As Rick Warren, an evangelical author and church-growth expert, wrote in *How to Preach Like Jesus,* "Effective salesmen know you always start with the customer, not the product."[4]

If you want to expand your church, we are told, find out what the seeker wants, then market Christianity as an answer to the seeker's "felt need." But should the desires of lost humanity be the center of Christianity? Is this seeker-friendly theology actually Biblical? How did Jesus present His Gospel?

Removing the Wrapper

Jesus clearly had a deep concern for people and their physical needs. He consistently showed compassion and concern for the "felt needs" of humanity. However, He made no attempt to soften truth or sugarcoat His message to please his listeners. When calling men to His kingdom, He started with the hard facts up front. "Whosoever he be of you that forsaketh not all that he hath, he cannot be my disciple."[e] is not a crowd-pleasing theme. It doesn't sound very seeker-friendly. But Jesus didn't come to please men; He came to do the will of His Father.[f]

When you make the seeker the center of Christianity, you are promoting something entirely different from Christ's message. Following Jesus is the answer to our troubled relationships, the cure for our obsession with wealth, and the ultimate source of eternal joy, but we have no promise that our earthly life will be more pleasurable when we choose to follow Him. Jesus and the early church taught the exact opposite. When people claiming to follow Jesus become seeker-centric instead of God-centric, they are promoting something the apostles would not have recognized.

The true Gospel has never been a comfortable message for the unconverted. It calls for drastic change, and many of us have been blessed to grow up in church settings that understand this. I grew up in a church where ministers taught against the fallacy of modern evangelical[g] Christianity. I was taught to "remove the wrapper" and look closer at what Jesus actually taught. Repeatedly I heard that many who call themselves Christians will be surprised at the judgment, and that just saying you believe in Jesus is not enough. I was confident that most churchgoers were only talking about Jesus, and I was thankful to be part of a church that was actually following

---

[e] Luke 14:33
[f] John 4:34, 8:29
[g] When referring to modern evangelical Christians throughout this book, I am referring to nominal modern Protestant Christianity.

Him. After all, we took Jesus' commands literally. Jesus had said we should wash each other's feet and love our enemies, and we believed that was exactly what He meant. Others made excuses, but we really did it. I liked that.

But there was one aspect I had not considered. Many of the modern churches I despised were actually imitating Jesus in one very important way that we were neglecting. They were burdened about the plight of the poor and the spiritual welfare of the lost.

At Least They Care About the Lost!

As I grew older and my exposure expanded, this began to trouble me. I read accounts of the Gospel spreading in restricted countries, people hearing about Jesus for the first time, and new first-generation churches springing up. God was obviously at work. Then it would hit me: these "modern evangelical Christians" were doing all this. How could this be?

I remember visiting a soup kitchen in the slums of a large American city. It was an old building full of dirty, dangerous, dysfunctional people. Occasional fights broke out, but around the edges of the room were people who were sick of sin and searching for something different. Ministering to them were dedicated, but doctrinally incorrect, Christians.

Once again I came face to face with an unsettling reality. These "modern evangelical Christians" were the ones venturing into this hazardous setting, dipping up soup, and listening to stories. Some of them may have been divorced and remarried. I knew I wouldn't agree with their position on serving in the military, and there were probably other basic teachings of Jesus they ignored. But one thing troubled me: they might not be correct on every doctrine, but they cared about the lost and downtrodden! They were not just talking about reaching out to people; they were out in the trenches, redemptively working with the strugglers society normally avoids.

Many of us who have grown up in conservative Anabaptist

churches have wrestled with similar questions. We are able to give a Scriptural answer for every conceivable question. Yet when we stand back and compare our local churches with those first believers in the book of Acts, something is often missing. Too many of us lack the vibrancy, passion, and power they possessed. Unlike those early believers, we struggle to get neighbors to visit our churches, and we seem incapable of impacting surrounding society as they did.

> Is it possible that we have all the right answers, but are asking the wrong questions?

While the churches in Acts were known for turning the world upside down, we have difficulty at times just holding our churches together. What is wrong? Is it possible that we have all the right answers, but are asking the wrong questions?

We talk about how churches should operate, which procedures are best, and even argue about independent churches versus conferences or fellowships. But too often we forget to investigate deeper. In this book we want to take a fresh look at the church. Why did God instigate the church in the first place? What did He have in mind? And now, centuries later, is it possible that we are on the wrong track?

CHAPTER TWO

Are We on the Right Track?

The New Testament contains much about the identity of the church, and I believe most of us are very aware of who we are. The church is a gathering of people who have been purchased with the blood of Jesus,[a] a called-out people who are holy,[b] a group of individuals living on earth whose names are written in heaven.[c] The church is Jesus' bride,[d] the pillar and ground of the truth,[e] and is described as the body of Christ.[f] That is who the church is. These truths are familiar and supported by passages we frequently hear. But sometimes it is easier to describe our identity than to articulate clear vision and purpose.

What We Are Not

Historically, churches have also been good at identifying what they are not. Many of us were raised with lists of things we don't do, clothing we don't wear, and places we don't go. We grew up understanding

---

[a] Acts 20:28
[b] Ephesians 5:27
[c] Hebrews 12:23
[d] Ephesians 5:23, Revelation 21:9
[e] 1 Timothy 3:15
[f] 1 Corinthians 12:27

that good Christians should not purchase certain products, should avoid frequent association with some people, and should abstain from certain stores and entertainments. We were taught the importance of good church standards that help us maintain separation from the world. We spend a great deal of time defining what we are not.

Even the larger evangelical church has frequently defined itself by what it stands against. Historically, the church has had a list of things that upstanding church members don't do. One hundred years ago it was common knowledge that Christians didn't smoke, drink, or dress immodestly. Churches taught that things like dancing, swearing, working on Sunday, and divorce were wrong. Those lists have changed. Many churches have joined forces with political parties, focusing on topics like abortion and gay marriage. Even churches that have gradually assimilated into surrounding culture tend to focus on what the church is against. It has been said that the church in America is the only organization in the world that defines itself more by what it doesn't do than what it actually does.

Where Are We Going?
Surely God had more in mind for His body than a group of people determining what shouldn't be done. Why did God want groups of people on the earth meeting, living, and working together? What are we supposed to be accomplishing? The theologian might respond, "We are to bring glory to God," and this is of course correct. The Apostle Paul was very clear about the ultimate goal of the church. Writing to the church at Ephesus, he said, "Unto him be glory in the church by Christ Jesus throughout all ages, world without end. Amen."[g] But what does this look like, and exactly how is a church to bring glory to God? By abstaining from certain things? If so, are those with the longest lists of rules bringing the most glory to God?

Obviously, if we are to bring glory to a holy God in our materialistic

---
[g] Ephesians 3:21

and self-centered culture, we will need to refrain from many things. Churches that fail to address the impact of society on their members will not last long. History has not been kind to fellowships that were unwilling to draw lines and hold their members accountable. But a parallel truth exists. Churches that develop a strong defense against the world, yet fail to embrace a love for their neighbors have not done well either. These churches tend to produce some strange anomalies.

In some very conservative churches, you may find individuals obeying the guidelines but giving themselves over to gossip, materialism, or an immoral thought life. You can find people in perfect compliance with their standards and rules, yet living very self-centered lives. They claim to follow Jesus, but in reality they are just having a good time.

Are We on the Right Track?

Recently I talked to a man who was discouraged. His church claims to imitate the One who came to seek and save those who are lost,[h] yet seems to have little interest in reaching out. His leaders have very little interaction with those outside their fellowship. He appreciates his church's caution but isn't sure this is what God has in mind for His church.

Was God's plan to have thousands of denominations, each putting its own spin on Christianity and focusing on what we shouldn't do? Young people watch others jump from church to church trying to find the "right" fellowship. They listen to discussions on worldliness, individualism, and the apparent lack of commitment. Sometimes their church seems like a powerful locomotive. The engine is running, smoke is coming out of the stack, and the wheels keep going around and around. Everything seems in order; it seems unstoppable and seems to be doing what trains are supposed to do. But is it going in the direction God had in mind? Is there a chance the church is on the wrong track?

---

[h] Luke 19:10

Several years ago I was traveling with my family, and on Sunday morning we visited a large non-denominational church. After the service a fellow worshiper introduced himself and asked what group I was affiliated with. I told him the name of our fellowship, and he abruptly concluded the conversation by saying, "We used to belong to a group like that too. We had lots of rules, but we got tired of all that. Now we come here where we don't have to think about rules and regulations. We can just focus on worshiping Jesus!" As we left the building and walked to the parking lot, his words replayed in my mind. Somewhere in this man's past he had experienced pain in working with fellow followers of Jesus. At some point, he had concluded it wasn't worth the struggle to learn from the past or plan for the future. He just wanted to worship Jesus in the present!

I have heard young people in our churches say similar things. They ask difficult questions: Why not avoid the conflicts, misunderstandings, and arguments about details? Why not just gather to hear good teaching, spend time worshiping God, and support evangelism programs? Why keep trying to submit to each other and blend lives with those who see things differently? Why not just forget all these rules and focus on introducing our neighbors to Jesus?

Do We Know Our Purpose?

Before we pitch church discipline, submission to authority, and accountability to a body of believers, shouldn't we back up and take a closer look at what God might have had in mind? Church life definitely would be easier without hard words like *submission*, but before we move on to an easier path, shouldn't we investigate God's purpose? After all, church was His idea!

I have noticed something about families experiencing financial struggles. They usually have tension in the home, insufficient funds in the bank account, and frustration with each other's financial decisions. They come asking for help, and their assumption is that the spouse is the problem and that a better budgeting system will take care of things. But rarely is their method of budgeting the real issue. Money simply follows our longings, and our longings flow from our purpose for life. When there is financial difficulty in a home, it is usually a result of no united vision. Until a couple has a united vision and purpose, there will always be conflict.

I believe the same is true of the church. Much of the conflict and confusion in local congregations is a result of failing to prayerfully establish direction and purpose.

What Is All This About?
The modern evangelical church has exhibited great concern for the unsaved, but has largely lost its way. Millions of dollars are being spent on outreach and missions, yet in its zeal to bring in the seeker, valuable doctrines have slipped away. It now acts like the world, looks like the world, and pursues the world's entertainment.

On the other side are the conservative churches that have stood firm against acculturation. They have taken seriously the command not to love the world and to be separate from it. Yet many of these churches have become so fixated on their internal needs and concerns that they have little interest in reaching out to their neighbors.

So are these the only two options? Is the church doomed to either be evangelistic and worldly, or separate but ineffective in sharing the Gospel with the world? Or is it possible that the church has been given the tools to be both evangelistic and separate, reaching out to neighbors in love without compromising a holy life in service to a holy God?

CHAPTER THREE

The Vibrant Church: A Coordinated Contradiction

For centuries medical students have studied human corpses, known as cadavers. We can read writings from several hundred years before Christ that describe men dissecting human bodies. But these early researchers had a problem. Cadavers begin to decay immediately after death, so there was little time to learn from them. Later, various embalming fluids were used to slow decay, and students today still use cadavers in their studies. Volunteers agree before death to let their preserved bodies be used to further education and research. Many living humans benefit from what has been learned by studying cadavers.

In 1977, Dr. Gunther von Hagens began pursuing another idea. He believed it should be possible to preserve bodies permanently, and he invented a process known as plastination. Using this process, a cadaver is infused with a polymer solution, allowing it to be studied and displayed indefinitely. He then began to exhibit the preserved bodies, allowing the public to marvel at the human body's amazing complexities. Today this traveling exhibition is known as Body Worlds, and millions of people have visited these exhibits in over a hundred cities around the world.[1]

Several years ago I had the opportunity to visit one of these displays. It is startling to walk into a room and see partially dissected human bodies posed as if performing various tasks. One man is swinging a baseball bat, with the inner parts of his arms and legs exposed to show how his muscles work. Another man is riding a bicycle, with his inner body exposed. Bones, muscles, tendons, inner organs—I couldn't help but pause in awe and wonder at how complex our bodies are, and yet how smoothly they work! The room was crowded but unusually quiet. People spoke in whispers, pointing and marveling at the intricacies of the human body.

A small sign in front of one of the displays caught my eye. The display was showing how muscles and bones work together in our arms and legs, and the sign said, "Every movement in the body requires a coordinated contradiction." Each time your arm or leg moves, a muscle is pulling one way while being resisted by a bone. The net result is movement. Assuming the brain coordinates things properly, this action is beneficial to the body. I left the Body Worlds exhibit that day thinking about this amazing statement: "Every movement in the body requires a coordinated contradiction." Take a moment and visualize what is happening when you raise your arm or move your leg. You are observing the marvel of bone and muscle working together to create movement.

Bone

Consider bone for a moment. Bone is rigid, unyielding, and sometimes limits what I want to do. If I reach for a glass of water three feet from my chair, my muscles can strain all they want, but my bones limit my reach. They keep my muscles from doing what they would like to do. Bones have no power by themselves, and skeletons alone are incapable of movement. Yet bones are important. A body without bones would be unable to support itself. Bones provide the stability needed to accomplish our daily tasks.

Muscle

Muscle is almost the exact opposite of bone. Flexible and elastic, muscle is willing to stretch and strain, trying to reach that glass of water. Muscle is also the source of power in our bodies. It is what young men like to flex as they grow, what they look at in the mirror as they gauge their growing strength. But if you have ever witnessed an athlete trying to get back on his feet after breaking a bone in his leg, you understand that muscle alone cannot do much. That man may be an Olympic runner with tremendous leg muscles, but without good bones in that leg to pull against, he's not going anywhere.

Muscle and bone have little in common. In fact, they seem to work against each other in our bodies and are in constant tension. Muscle is flexible and constantly pulling against the bone. Bone is inflexible and always bracing against muscle. Yet when bone and muscle work together as God intended, each getting instruction from the brain, it is a beautiful sight. As the sign in the Body Worlds exhibit stated, it is a coordinated contradiction. Meaningful tasks are accomplished because members of the body are working together in a coordinated way and for a specific purpose. Muscle by itself cannot do it, and neither can bone. But out of the strain and stress of muscle pulling against bone, and bone restricting the movement of muscle, great things are accomplished. Who but God could ever have created this marvelous arrangement?

The Body of Christ

The Apostle Paul, writing to the church at Corinth, used the human body as an analogy for the church. Our bodies are made up of many extremely diverse members, and Paul says, "But now hath God set the members every one of them in the body, as it hath pleased him."[a] God knows that muscle and bone are very different, yet he expects them to work harmoniously. He has also placed people with differing personality traits and natural abilities in our churches, and He expects them to work together smoothly just as our bodies do.

Church Bones

As I look at our churches, I see some members who are like bones. They love structure and stability, and resist movement. They are consistent and predictable. When a suggestion comes before the brotherhood, they like to go back to history and try to learn from errors in the past. They think long-term, asking where each path might lead. The "bones" see the errors of the modern evangelical church and provide much-needed stability.

But they also have some weaknesses. The "bones" tend to rely so heavily on experience that it is difficult for them to visualize a new path. When God commanded the Israelites to cross the Red Sea, I suspect there were some who were concerned. They had never seen God work that way before. At times the "bones" of a church are terrified by change and can keep a church from living to its full potential. They can be fearful of outreach and concerned that too much interaction with society will impact the church's holiness.

Church Muscles

I also see individuals in our churches who could be considered muscles. They love action and spiritual life and want to see more movement. They are flexible and like to see things happen. When a suggestion comes before the brotherhood that threatens to restrict movement, they will often ask why we don't trust people more. They talk about the need for spiritual revival and the importance of fasting and prayer. The "muscles" in a church provide much-needed enthusiasm, life, and spiritual focus. They love to remind the church that

---

[a] 1 Corinthians 12:18

there is higher ground and that we can do better.

But "muscles" also have some weaknesses. They love spontaneity in church life and see little need for history. Sometimes in their desire to evangelize, "muscles" get too close to the world. After all, souls are going to hell! Why worry about insignificant details of dress or other cultural trends? They see little need for structure and brotherhood agreements. After all, if a church just listens to the Spirit, how can it go wrong? At times the "muscles" can become stifled by stability, longing for change without considering long-term ramifications.

Very few of us, if any, could be classified as wholly bone or wholly muscle. Most of us are a combination. Yet as you read across these two categories, certain people likely came to mind. God intended that both be a blessing to the body of Christ.

Church Divisions

What happens when bone and muscle separate? If your leg muscle disconnects from your bone, can you go to work or achieve the goals you have set for the day? Of course not. When muscle and bone separate, coordinated movement stops. There may be some thrashing around on the ground, but meaningful, purposeful action stops.

I want to suggest the same is true in the church. Look at history. Many church divisions slice right between bone and muscle. Think of the church splits you have observed. How many were over actual false doctrine, and how many were simply muscle and bone concluding they were too incompatible to go on together? Where did we get the idea that churches will be stronger by dissecting muscle and bone? This has occurred so often that it has become normal, as though division is the natural and predictable end of long-term church life.

So Pastor Bone starts a new church on one side of the road, and Pastor Muscle on the other. Based on history, Pastor Bone predicts that the Muscle-ites will drift closer and closer to the world. Yes, they might have more visitors, and a few of them might join. But over time they will begin to look like the surrounding culture until there is little difference between them and the world. Pastor Bone is right. History repeats itself.

Pastor Muscle also makes some predictions. He has always said a church that focuses primarily on history, rather than on the Bible and the Spirit of God, will die from within. Everything might look good on the outside, but over time it will decay inside. He predicts that the Bone-ites will become even more rigid and uncaring about the lost and will have less and less interest in reaching out in the community. Pastor Muscle, too, is right. Now both console themselves by looking at the flaws in the other.

Major Differences

Diversity exists in every church. There are differences in personalities. Some people are very organized and live by lists. Others would immediately forget where they put the list if they ever actually made one. Some are outgoing and love to communicate. Others prefer solitude. Some visualize a vibrant church as spontaneous, while others become uncomfortable outside a predictable environment. Some would like a social function every night and assume there must be something wrong with those who like to stay home. The list could go on.

There are also major differences in our past experiences. Some have been wounded by cold legalism, while others grew up in spiritual chaos and now desire a structured environment. Some were raised in godly homes where the Scriptures were read each day, and prayer and fasting were normal. Others have little or no experience of faith within their homes. Some emerged from their teenage years with very few scars, and others have memories they wish they could erase. The list of diversity in past experiences could go on and on. But all of these things have a dramatic impact on how we view the church. Differences in natural abilities, personalities, and experience produce varying perspectives and differing expectations from church. So how do we draw such a diverse group of people into a unified, effective church body?

Three Options

I suggest that we have three primary options in dealing with the diversity of gifts God has placed in His body.

1. **Ignoring Diversity.** Churches that follow this path tend to focus on exhaustive Bible study, praise, and worship while ignoring diversity in the body. They intentionally circumvent the painful process of addressing differences and agreeing on collective application of Scriptural principles. They let each person decide what he feels the Bible is telling him. This is very common in modern evangelical Christianity. But if a local church is going to function as a body, it will need to discuss its differences. When God's Spirit fills a man, he will have a strong desire to unite with other believers. His desire for the greater good will be stronger than love for his own opinion. A church that avoids commitment and the self-denying love required to blend lives will never be able to demonstrate self-sacrificing love to a self-centered, dysfunctional world.

2. **Death by Dissection.** Separate the gifts; put the muscle in one church and the bone in the church down the road. Most of us are familiar with this approach, and maybe this option is best if you believe the only goal of the church is self-preservation and perpetuation. But if you believe God wants the church to be a public demonstration of Jesus Christ, can you imagine the pain this dissection brings to the Father? Few events declare a lack of love for Jesus and His passion for unity like a church split. We are essentially shouting to the local community, "The Gospel of Jesus Christ is powerful, but not powerful enough to overcome our personality differences and self-centeredness." Don't expect visitors from the community immediately after a church division.

3. **A Coordinated Contradiction.** God has given us a human body as a beautiful example of how His church is to operate. The different personalities and natural abilities existing in our churches are not there by accident. God is intentional as He builds each church, and He has "set the members every one of them in the body, as it hath pleased him."[b] It is easy to read that verse, but do you really believe it? What about that brother who always seems to restrict your movement and squelch every good idea? Or that sister who always has a new idea and wants to change the way things are done? Perhaps God has intentionally placed them on the pew beside you, not to hinder His work, but to enable the body to move forward.

We are called to self-denying love as we work in concert with those whose gifts, pasts, and personalities are different from ours. We are not called to just coexist. Any worldly organization can accomplish that. Instead, we are called to lay down our rights and desires, to see God's purpose in those who see things differently, and then to work in unison toward a greater good.

But what is this greater good? What did God actually have in mind when He placed people with different temperaments and diverse natural abilities into churches? In short, what is God's overriding purpose?

> We are not called to just coexist. Any worldly organization can accomplish that.

---

[b] 1 Corinthians 12:18

CHAPTER FOUR

Church: What Did God Have in Mind?

It is late in the summer of 1741, and in a small London house on Brook Street a man sits hunched over his desk, writing industriously. He has been here for days, rarely even stopping to eat. It has been three weeks since he left his home. There is good reason for his diligence: he is drowning in debt, and many are saying his work as a music composer is over.

He has experienced some wonderful days in his past—times when British monarchs and wealthy audiences believed he was the greatest. Yet his fortunes have changed for the worse. The bills are accumulating, the adoring audiences are gone, and debtor's prison looms.

A servant carrying a tray of food pauses just outside his door. He wonders if it's even worth the bother. Repeatedly he has brought meals to his eccentric employer, only to return later and find the most tempting dishes untouched. Knocking softly, he opens the door, steps into the room, and pauses. The composer turns, tears streaming down his face, and cries out, "I did think I did see all heaven before me, and the great God Himself!"[1]

George Handel had just finished writing the *Messiah*. It filled 260 pages of manuscript, and musical experts today still marvel that Handel could complete such a large undertaking in just twenty-four days.

Hundreds of years later, audiences are still moved by this inspiring music. One biographer of Handel said, "Considering the immensity of the work and the short time involved, it will remain, perhaps forever, the greatest feat in the whole history of music composition."[2] The heading for the project was as understated as the music was complex. George simply called it *Messiah,* and at the end of the manuscript wrote the letters "SDG." These initials stood for *Soli Deo Gloria,* or "To God alone the glory."

Messiah, first performed in Dublin on April 13, 1742, was quickly recognized as a stunning piece of music. King George was reportedly so moved that he stood during the finale, the "Hallelujah Chorus," obliging all to stand with him. This tradition of standing during the chorus has continued to this day. While there is no direct evidence that King George started this longstanding tradition, those who listen to the *Messiah* testify that it connects with something deep within the human heart. There is something triumphant and redemptive in the music itself that makes the listener want to stand. When performed well, the *Messiah* causes the listener to feel he has come close to "the great God Himself!"

Power in Music

There is no question: music is capable of moving men. From the teen bobbing his head and snapping his fingers at a stoplight to the urge to stand during the "Hallelujah Chorus," something in music makes us want to move. It has been used to call soldiers to bravery, incite punk rockers to rebellion, and motivate the discouraged. When George Handel originally wrote the *Messiah,* that was his intent. He was not randomly scribbling music on paper. Every measure, note, and word was designed to move people.

I suggest that God intentionally designed the church for the same purpose. Persuasive music should flow out of our churches—harmonious music that moves the listener. Those in our communities who constantly observe our choices, our love for each other, and our daily lives should be moved to see "the great God Himself!"

New Testament Music

Recently a foreign visitor who was seeking truth came to our local church. This college student had been attending various churches in our area for several years, trying to learn about Christianity. As we discussed her overall impression of the congregations in our town, she made this statement: "Christian people seem to be very nice and helpful, but also very disconnected from each other." She went on to say that they were focused on doctrine and wanted to teach her why their dogma was superior to others. However, there seemed to be little meaningful interaction between members.

"In my country, people love to sit, talk, and just be together. Here, Christian people can explain their beliefs about Jesus, but they seem very detached. They sit through a service and then get up and go home. They don't seem to have time for each other." The "music" they were producing wasn't attractive. Hearing continual debate on doctrine was not moving her to follow Jesus.

It is easy for us to study, debate, and defend our doctrinal differences, but God intended so much more! The New Testament, like a piece of sheet music, is not something just to be analyzed, studied, and debated. It is something to be played! God intends that we take the teachings of Jesus, apply them in our churches, and produce music that is convincing and compelling. In the middle of a self-centered world, the melody coming out of a loving, caring, compassionate church is a beautiful thing. But this will be

> The New Testament, like a piece of sheet music, is not something just to be analyzed, studied, and debated. It is something to be played!

accomplished only if there is harmony.

Music That Moves People

What is it about music that moves us? When people stand during the "Hallelujah Chorus," why do they feel inspired? Is it the toot of the trumpet, the clash of the cymbals, or the powerful quality of the baritone's voice? Or maybe the skill of an expert violinist who has practiced for years and mastered his instrument until it seems like an extension of his body? As people listen, is there a single instrument creating that desire within to rise and do better? No, it's not any one component. Rather, people are inspired when they hear a well-composed piece with each musician playing in harmony.

The same is true in our churches. When each member connects to the Holy Spirit, plays his part, and aims to bring glory to God, it is beautiful and compelling. Churches like this produce music that moves people. Notice this statement regarding the early church (or perhaps we should call it the orchestra of Jesus Christ). "And all that believed were together, and had all things common; and sold their possessions and goods, and parted them to all men, as every man had need. And they, continuing daily with one accord in the temple, and breaking bread from house to house, did eat their meat with gladness and singleness of heart."[a] Notice in this description of the early church how many of the words speak of unity. Words like *together, common,* and *of one accord.* Like a beautiful orchestra, the church was working together, and the music produced was persuasive. In the next verse it says, "The Lord added to the church daily such as should be saved."[b] As they worked in concert with each other through the power of the Spirit, people were moved.

---

[a] Acts 2:44–46
[b] Acts 2:47

So often we forget the power of harmony. Visualize for a moment an orchestra in which each player is intent on demonstrating the superiority of his instrument. Try to imagine the sounds that would emanate from a group of musicians who disregarded the conductor, trying to outdo each other. The trombonist, fearful of not being noticed, is scarlet-faced as he blares his best tones. The soloists, not to be outdone, break forth in song whenever there's an opening. The audience would not only be standing, it would be heading for the door!

If our churches are to produce music that moves a seeker to the kingdom of God, the members must play in harmony. You can have the best preaching, the nicest building, and the most melodious singing, but if a visitor senses discord in your congregation, he will soon move on. Don't expect a visitor to return if members are more interested in their own tunes than in working together and producing a melody in concert with the Conductor.

Doctrinal Debate

If an orchestra is to produce good harmony, the members must become familiar with the music itself. They will need to study the notes, give thought to timing, and have a good grasp of the composer's musical notations. They must understand musical scales, chords, and rhythm. An orchestra whose members are not interested in learning these things would not be worth listening to.

Now imagine an orchestra that became fixated on studying the notes. Twice a week they meet and closely review their sheet music. Some have memorized large sections of the music, and sometimes they gather to talk about the importance of memorization. Other times they review the composer's intent, and occasionally they discuss the faults of other orchestras. Gravely they sit, shake their heads in dismay, and wonder how other orchestras can be so far off on their timing or how they can consistently miss certain notes. This group has a tremendous understanding of music, but despite their expertise, they never actually produce any music.

Can you imagine an orchestra like this? One that focuses on

musical accuracy instead of playing the music? How many people would want to gather and listen? How much interest would there be?

God has provided the Bible to guide and direct His church, and He intends that we study it and try to discern His intent. But ultimately, He wants us to live it out. If all my church does is gather each Lord's Day and talk about the music, review its perfection, and agree that our understanding is better than that of others, what does God think? Our world is full of false teaching, and it is essential that our churches have sound doctrine. To a seeker, however, we sometimes resemble an orchestra obsessed with notes and timing, yet failing to produce harmonious chords.

A Sanctified Symphony

It is God's intent for His church to move people. Each congregation, regardless of how small, should be a public demonstration of Jesus Christ, not just because it has good doctrine or members who can properly articulate their beliefs, but because it applies Jesus' teachings in daily life. We are to be a public performance on the stage of life, producing compelling music that convicts every serious seeker and causes him to consider the original Composer.

When George Handel sat down to write the *Messiah*, he had a goal. For three weeks he focused on timing, melody, and creating dramatic chords. Yet his vision was much higher than just good music. His goal was to move people.

God also has a goal. The Bible has wonderful poetry and remarkable consistency throughout. It has been written in a way that cuts to the heart. Yet beyond all this, it has an overriding purpose we sometimes forget: it is the sheet music for daily life in His church. God desires a melody produced by blood-bought saints who truly love each other, and harmony coming from believers who are willing to surrender their own desires for the greater cause. When this occurs, a compelling harmony will come from our churches—music that cannot be found anywhere else in the world!

CHAPTER FIVE

What Kind of Music Is Your Church Producing?

All of us want churches that inspire people. We desire congregations that exhibit the redemptive power of God in daily life. We would like to work harmoniously with fellow believers, publicly demonstrating the love of Jesus. We want beautiful, powerful music to come from our local congregations. But there is a problem: "doing church" is hard work.

It all begins so nicely. A group professing to love Jesus starts meeting together. The people get along well and enjoy peace and harmony. Then some time passes and little disagreements arise. Suspicions develop as personalities surface and strong statements are made. Eventually, this group of well-meaning people feels unable to fellowship with each other. They separate, each subgroup believing its perspective is superior and worth defending. Every group believes it has a good understanding of where God desires the church to walk. And all profess to be following the One who taught us to love each other and esteem others better than ourselves. Amazing! We can articulate Bible doctrines, testify of God's work in our lives, and even verbalize our great love for each other. Yet we seem incapable of walking together very long without conflict.

Take a cursory glance over church history. Some of the most intense and violent times have been centered on disagreements about God or how He wants His church to be administrated. Men have imprisoned other men, exiled them to distant islands, and even burned fellow Christians at the stake. The path of church history seems littered with stories of ecclesiastical divorce. Someone once wrote:

> *To dwell in love with saints above,*
> *Why, that will be glory.*
> *To dwell below with saints I know,*
> *Why, that's a different story.*

Doing church is difficult, and seekers become discouraged by continual dissonance. But let's bring this a little closer. How is this playing out in your congregation? Are you producing compelling New Testament music? As honest seekers listen to the music floating from the daily lives of your congregation, are they attracted to the harmony or repelled by discordant notes?

God's Overriding Purpose

Throughout the Bible we find God repeatedly interacting with His creation. He does it in different ways at different times, but why? What is His end goal? As I read the Bible, I see two primary purposes.

The first is to reveal His majesty to the world. Walk outside on a dark clear night and look up. The stars are shouting His glory! David said, "The heavens declare the glory of God; and the firmament sheweth his handiwork."[a] Walk through the forest and look at the plant life, examine the great diversity of animal life, or peer at pond water under a microscope. Anywhere you choose to look, God is proclaiming and revealing His glory. That is one of His purposes for interacting with His creation.

A second way God wants to be glorified is by bringing man back

---

[a] Psalm 19:1

to Himself, a far more difficult job. While speaking the universe into existence took less than a week, reconciling rebellious humanity to Himself through redemption has been going on much longer. Ultimately, redeeming man will manifest His glory as well, but for a moment consider the effort God has expended in His desire to reconcile us to Himself. The Bible tells us of three major moves God made to bring about redemption. Notice God's overriding desire and how this affects our local church.

A Great Nation

We find the first move to reconcile man to Himself early in the Bible. God told Abraham, "I will make of thee a great nation, and I will bless thee, and make thy name great; and thou shalt be a blessing."[b] God tells how this will happen and ends by saying, "And in thee shall all families of the earth be blessed."[c] Notice, God was not going to bless Abraham and his descendants so they could just enjoy life. God also had His eye on the rest of the world. He had a greater purpose behind blessing Israel. This must have been difficult for Israel to remember. Moses had to remind them just before they entered the Promised Land that God was going to bless them "and all people of the earth shall see that thou art called by the name of the LORD."[d] This purpose is woven throughout the Old Testament. Psalm 67 says, "God be merciful unto us, and bless us; and cause his face to shine upon us." Why? "That thy way may be known upon earth, thy saving health among all nations."[e] God blessed Israel so the entire world would observe and turn to Him.

The Incarnation

The second major move to redeem, as shown in Scripture, is the incarnation of Jesus Christ. Jesus came as a King to save His own

---

[b] Genesis 12:2
[c] Genesis 12:3, 22:18
[d] Deuteronomy 28:10
[e] Psalm 67:1, 2

people.[f] He was very clear about His mission. When asked by a desperate Gentile mother to heal her sick daughter, Jesus responded, "I am not sent but unto the lost sheep of the house of Israel."[g] Yet we see little glimpses all through the life of Jesus that His purpose was much broader than just reaching the nation of Israel. One of the most recited passages of the Christian faith, spoken by Jesus Himself, states clearly, "Whosoever believeth in Him should not perish, but have everlasting life."[h] Jesus came to save His own people, but His eye was also on redeeming the rest of the world.

The Church

God's final effort in redemption, found in the New Testament, is the church. The Apostle Paul calls this a great mystery that even the great prophets of the past could not have conceived or imagined.[i] As we read Paul's letter to the church at Ephesus, he seems to be trying to wrap his mind around this staggering truth—that God, who has all power and ability, would place His reputation in the hands of ordinary men and women and allow them to display His character and attributes. No wonder Paul was mystified! Using weak, self-centered, unreliable men to demonstrate a powerful, loving, and changeless God? No wonder men in past ages didn't see this coming!

Paul continues drawing parallels with things the believers at Ephesus could understand. He talks about a great mystery hidden from the beginning of the world.[j] He compares the close connection between members in the church to joints and ligaments in human anatomy. But his most powerful analogy is that of a marriage between husband and wife. Though this passage is rightly used for instruction in marriage ceremonies, we often forget that the primary purpose of this teaching is not for marriage. It is to teach God's design for His church.

---

[f] John 1:11
[g] Matthew 15:24
[h] John 3:16
[i] Ephesians 3:3–6
[j] Ephesians 3:9

God desires good marriages, but the picture here is of church members so closely connected, so self-denying, so purposeful in their love and commitment to each other that God can put them on display. Their oneness and love for each other is to demonstrate the majesty of God. Try to comprehend His vision! God desires that people looking at our churches see something so compelling, so powerful, so earth-shatteringly different from anything else that they immediately sense God's presence!

> God desires that people looking at our churches see something so compelling, so powerful, so earth-shatteringly different from anything else that they immediately sense God's presence!

Jesus told His disciples, "By this shall all men know that ye are my disciples, if ye have love one to another."[k] God gives us continual opportunities in our churches to show love. Some of us are difficult to get along with, some repeatedly make poor choices, and all of us say things we shouldn't. We disappoint each other and fail to live up to the expectations we set for each other. Basically, we are made out of the same stuff everyone else is. Yet we are called, through the power of Jesus Christ within, to exhibit something entirely different.

I marvel at God's persistence in redemption. He blessed Israel, and they repeatedly failed Him. God sent Jesus, and He was mocked, despised, and crucified. Finally, the church was empowered to deliver the Gospel and demonstrate the love of God to a lost world. Looking back at church history can make us scratch our heads. Is this really what God had in mind? Yet God knew all this from the

---

[k] John 13:35

very beginning. No wonder Paul concludes by saying that God's use of ordinary people working together to illustrate His love is a "great mystery!"[l] It also seems like an extremely risky venture!

What Are Seekers Seeing?

Most of us are verbally delivering the Gospel in some way. You may even have a sign in front of your church welcoming visitors. But are you collectively demonstrating the character and person of Jesus Christ? Is that what people see when they visit? Or are they even visiting?

Recently a brother expressed concern about the lack of visitors in his congregation. It had been a long time since anyone from his community had visited. After discussing this he remarked, "Americans have plenty of food, nice houses, and an abundance of entertainment options. It just doesn't seem like anyone in America is interested in the Gospel anymore." Do you agree? Is that the only reason people are not hungry for the Gospel? Obviously, people who are satiated with pleasure and plenty will have less interest in spiritual things. But are we sure there is no spiritual hunger in America and that a lack of visitors on Sunday morning is due to disinterest?

Make no mistake. Many people were not interested in the self-denying message Jesus brought. If they walked away from Jesus, we can expect the same. But we must analyze our churches to figure out if people are disinterested for the same reasons they weren't interested in Jesus' message. Men like the rich young ruler rejected Jesus because the cost was too high.[m] What about our churches? If our neighbors aren't interested, is it because we are portraying the message of Jesus so clearly that they recognize the high cost of discipleship? Or are serious seekers staying away for some other reason?

Let's look at a few reasons seekers might lose interest.

Church: Where Music Is Analyzed

It is possible for churches to study the New Testament each week,

---

[l] Ephesians 5:32
[m] Matthew 19:16–22

yet put little emphasis on application. Of course, few of us see this trait in ourselves, but in a time when education is extolled and self-denial avoided, it isn't difficult to slip into this mode. It is amazing how well we can study Greek origins, chase down root words, and read commentaries, yet be unable to think of a time in the last month when the Word of God altered our daily lives. A. W. Tozer once asked, "At what point, then, does a theological fact become for the one who holds it a life-giving truth? At the point where obedience begins."[1] If the Word of God is not moving us, how can we hope to move people in our community?

Church: Where Orchestras of the Past Are Revered

I enjoy reading history. Individuals and churches have done astounding things in the past, and there is much to be learned. Yet churches can become more excited about praising past performances than producing compelling music today. We can focus on the early church, talk about martyrs during the Reformation, or extol church leaders who lived thirty years ago. But the music coming out of a church living in the past will have little to offer the serious seeker today. If you find yourself more interested in church history than in the struggling single mother who lives down the street, don't expect her to visit your church.

Church: Praising the Composer Instead of Performing the Music

One of the popular themes in modern evangelical Christianity is "gathering to exalt the name of Jesus." "Praise the Lord!" seems almost a buzz phrase, and in many churches, praise time consumes over half of the service. This sounds like a wonderful thing. Surely we can't spend too much time praising Jesus!

A few years ago in China, a house church leader told me, "You Christians in America have made an idol out of Jesus!" Surprised, I asked him for an explanation. He said Americans love to gather each week and talk about Jesus. They write love songs about Jesus, and singers get up in front and croon into the microphone, telling how

43

much Jesus means to them. But then they go back out to their daily lives, ignoring what He said to do. The church leader said that is exactly how people worship idols in his country. It is much easier to exalt the Lord in our song service than to do what He says.

> It is much easier to exalt the Lord in our song service than to do what He says.

Church: Only Trumpets Allowed?

Jesus was clear that He came to save whosoever will,[n] but that is not the perception surrounding many churches today. I have heard many seekers ask if a person needs to be born into an Anabaptist church to be a member there. Perhaps even worse is the low retention rate of those who are serious enough to visit and eventually join. Many can tell of the initial joy of joining. They came wanting more—more focus on the Bible, more community, and more spiritual vitality. But after a few years of submitting to rules they don't understand, listening to continual faultfinding of other groups, and observing carnality in areas not addressed in the churches rules, they leave. They are no longer sure that their change was an upgrade.

Many come from fellowships that had spiritual life but were ignoring some basic doctrines. Sometimes people who make this change feel they gained a few correct doctrines but lost the spiritual vitality. When a minister speaks disparagingly about the people who originally brought them to the Lord, it becomes discouraging. It is like the trumpet players in the orchestra continually speaking ill of the saxophone players. Maybe the saxophonists are missing some notes, but can't the trumpeters just focus on perfecting their own role in the orchestra?

Leo Tolstoy once said, "Everyone thinks of changing the world, but

---

[n] John 3:16

no one thinks of changing himself."[2] The same is true for churches. It is easier for churches to talk about the great problems in modern evangelical Christianity than to face glaring realities at home.

Bringing It Home

We live in a fragmented society. People feel unloved, unaccepted, and alone, and vast amounts of money and time are being spent trying to fill an inner void. Many are filling their lives with entertainment and sports, while others search for fulfillment through social media, chat rooms, and other online forums. Something inside longs for connection. Yet in spite of all this effort, there has never been a more socially disconnected society. Something vital is missing.

God longs to fill that inner void in every human heart with His own presence, and He designed loving church communities to demonstrate His love to dysfunctional and lonely people. Church should be a place where the disconnected can connect, but this can only occur when believers sacrificially love each other. When tension and conflict characterize a local church, one can hardly expect the seeker to grasp the true nature of God or develop a curiosity about Christ.

The need around us is great, and it is time for each of us to analyze what kind of music our congregation is producing.

PART TWO

CHURCH and CULTURE

CHAPTER SIX

When the Symphony Goes Sour

Just before going to the cross, Jesus prayed, "I pray not that thou shouldest take them out of the world, but that thou shouldest keep them from the evil."[a] Since that time, the church has wrestled with just how we are to interact with the world. We know we are to be different from society, but how? Sincere followers of Jesus see this question from different perspectives. We come from different backgrounds and have different personalities. But something else affects this tension as well: our differing gifts given by God Himself.

In chapter three we looked at the function of muscle and bone and the strain that develops in a church when those with different gifts fail to see the blessing in the others. Often this tension surrounds the question of how much influence the surrounding culture should have on our lives. Disagreement over this question can destroy the harmonious music that should be coming from our churches. Let's look at its impact on the fictional Shady Oak congregation.

---
[a] John 17:15

Problems at Shady Oak

Tension filled the air as each member considered the problem at hand. It had been avoided for some time, but due to growing unrest in the Shady Oak congregation, something had to be done. As in many conflicts, two men with different viewpoints were at the forefront of the struggle. To an onlooker it was a small matter, just a question of dress among some of the younger sisters. Changes had come gradually, and the ministry could not agree on how to respond.

To Pastor Neidmor Outreach, the problem was obvious. He saw the church as an active mission to the world. The Shady Oak church was surrounded by unbelievers, and yet the congregation was so focused on rules that there was little time to think about the lost. Why sit around discussing clothing details when people were lost? Pastor Neidmor was weary of all this talk about drift. Why not trust fellow members and allow the Lord to work in their lives? Righteousness couldn't be legislated anyway! Neidmor Outreach tried to listen as others spoke, but a great burden pressed on his heart: "Why don't we show greater concern for our neighbors?"

Sitting across the table was Pastor Firmon Tradition, and the problem at Shady Oak was apparent to him as well. There was simply too much love for the world in their congregation. The fact that these issues about dress kept coming up indicated a deeper problem, and a brief look at history would quickly prove this. Churches that neglected to maintain their agreements drifted into worldliness and carnality. How could a church be a light to the world when it was no different than the world? As Firmon Tradition listened, a question kept circling around his mind: "Why can't we learn from history?"

Sorrowful Separation

One year later the Shady Oak congregation underwent a painful church split. About half of its members went with Pastor Tradition and the other half followed Pastor Outreach. Firmon Tradition's congregation tried to get back on good solid footing. They had learned their lesson and concluded that agreements were extremely important. Firmon's church attracted the members from Shady Oak who were stable and cautious. While they occasionally talked about reaching out to the lost, no one was very passionate about it.

Neidmor Outreach's church did not make any immediate changes. They just agreed that their emphasis had been too self-centered. They wanted more than legalism and a focus on preservation. There was a lost world out there, and they felt called to reach out within their community. While they still professed a desire to live a counterculture life, it soon became obvious that separation from the world was not a high priority.

Ten Years Later

Firmon Tradition had assumed that separating from the worldly members would solve the church's problems, and for a time it did relieve some stress. But in his quiet times he wondered if another route could have been better. As he thought of his congregation, he wished more members were interested in spiritual things. Some of them were good at complying with agreements, yet he wasn't sure how much spiritual vitality lay underneath. He was painfully aware that a man could live a very carnal life while being alert and obedient to church standards. He also wondered why they had so few converts from the community. But one fact gave Pastor Tradition great satisfaction. His church had not drifted toward the world like Pastor Outreach's church had!

Neidmor Outreach had hoped that separating from a legalistic focus would solve his church's problems, and for a while it did make things easier. But at times he wondered just how much his church had gained. As he looked out over his congregation, he wondered why the members were so susceptible to every passing fashion. He wished there were more separation from the world. Some of his members were even losing their interest in reaching out to their neighbors, and he wondered about their spiritual health. He was brought face to face with an uncomfortable reality. A man can live a very carnal life, all the while soothing his conscience with an occasional mission trip. But one thing provided Neidmor some consolation. His church did not seem as legalistic and dead as Firmon Tradition's!

What Went Wrong?

Firmon Tradition and Neidmor Outreach were both godly men. They both had, and still have, an intense desire to follow God and be good shepherds to their flocks. Neidmor didn't want his church to lose its separation from the world, and Firmon really wanted to see converts from the community. But in the end neither arrived at the destination they desired. Why not?

Firmon Tradition left Shady Oak followed by individuals who were serious about separation from the world. They were concerned about drift and wanted a church that was willing to take a stand against worldliness. They were Bible readers, very aware of God's desire for a separate people. They loved verses like, "Wherefore come out from among them, and be ye separate."[b]

But some others had followed Firmon Tradition to his new congregation. These were people with hidden carnality in their hearts. Firmon was not aware of this, and perhaps these individuals were not aware either. They found church rules and structure an excellent protection against the call of the Spirit to higher ground. They were uncomfortable when called upon to pray in public, participate in a group Bible study, or share their thoughts on a sermon. They had little interest in having their spiritual lives and level of holiness

---

[b] 2 Corinthians 6:17

challenged. They found their satisfaction and confidence in abiding by the rules of the church.

Neidmor Outreach also left Shady Oak followed by individuals who were serious about following God. They carried a strong burden for the lost and wanted a church that was serious about reaching out. They were Bible readers, aware of God's desire for the lost. They loved verses like, "Go ye therefore, and teach all nations, baptizing them in the name of the Father, and of the Son, and of the Holy Ghost: teaching them to observe all things whatsoever I have commanded you."[c]

Neidmor Outreach also had some people whose motives were not as pure as he had originally hoped. Some of them used talk about evangelism as a protection against the Biblical call to holiness. They didn't seem to appreciate hearing about the importance of separation from the world. Neidmor was also concerned as he observed the women becoming more distracted by the latest styles, and the men discussing the latest sports scores more often. Yet he would overhear his congregation rejoicing in their avoidance of legalism and their occasional involvement in an evangelistic endeavor.

While Shady Oak is fictitious, this scenario has been played out repeatedly in the Christian church. In fact, it is so common that most of us can visualize several situations where something like this has taken place. Many of us can tell a similar story. Beyond the many seekers who get lost in these separations, what about the church youth who become discouraged and lose their way? Some become legalistic, concluding that constant doctrinal battles are proof that they are involved in Christian warfare. Others, weary of the strife, become disillusioned with separation or church agreements and turn to other professing Christian churches for relief. *At least there isn't continual conflict in churches with little structure and few rules,* they think.

---

[c] Matthew 28:19, 20

Losing Sight of Our Purpose

All of us are aware that God has a strong desire that all men be saved.[d] We know God intends His church to proclaim the Gospel to a lost world. Most churches would say, "Our goal is to reach out to the lost." So why do churches struggle to work collectively toward this goal?

I suggest there are two basic reasons. First, we forget the underlying evangelistic purpose of unity within the body of Christ. Jesus did not instruct us to live in harmony for our own pleasure. He wanted us to become one "that the world may believe."[e] Harmonious music coming from the local church connects with the deepest longings within seekers and draws them to Him.

Second, too many men like Neidmor Outreach and Firmon Tradition fail to see the blessing the other is bringing to the body of Christ. They forget that God has sent the other to offset their own deficiency, and that muscle and bone complement each other. They both agree that God has something more glorious than what they are experiencing, yet they cannot agree on how change should occur and which direction it should take. As we will see in the next few chapters, the way they view this present world and surrounding culture is at the heart of their disagreement.

---

[d] 1 Timothy 2:3, 4
[e] John 17:21

CHAPTER SEVEN

The Challenge of Culture

My father was born into a rural Indiana community in 1921. Growing up on a small farm during the Great Depression, little thought was given to anything except work and survival. It took everyone's hard labor to keep the farm going. But at the end of the day they made time for one sport. Like most Indiana boys, my father and his brothers loved basketball. The barn floor was rough and the lighting dim, but they loved the challenge of competing against each other to get the ball through the hoop.

Basketball was a major sport at the public school my father attended. Those talented enough to be on the team were the envy of their classmates. Many boys practiced after their evening chores, hoping to qualify for the team. One young man in the school had exceptional ability. My father remembered watching in awe as he swished the ball through the hoop time after time. In spite of his talent, this young man was never allowed to be on the school team. He had been seen smoking a cigarette after school hours and was barred from competing. My father also spoke about a teacher in his school who was seen smoking in town after school hours. He was dismissed immediately. The school board didn't want teachers who were poor role models for students.

Listening to my father forty years later, I was amazed. My world was totally different. Stories like this might have been normal in my father's day, but to my young ears in the 1970s, they sounded like messages from a different planet. Smoking after hours? My local high school was dealing with issues like teen pregnancy, violence, and substance abuse. The use of drugs was so common in the public schools that staff were hired just to monitor the use of narcotics and make sure students didn't overdose on illegal substances. Smoking cigarettes was of little concern. Schools where I grew up had designated smoking areas where students could smoke and relax. My father and I grew up in the same country, but in just a few decades the cultural mindset had shifted drastically.

My father's world leaned heavily on Judeo-Christian values. He didn't attend a Christian school, yet there was Bible reading and prayer before class. Certain activities, such as smoking, were deemed culturally wrong for upstanding citizens. But in my world, coming out of the hippie movement of the late 1960s, that Biblical foundation was being tested and in many cases discarded. This greatly affected people's view of what was normal.

Culture

Culture is a way of thinking, behaving, and working, and it exists in every people group. It affects everything—art, housing, clothes, and the food we eat. The reason you eat cornflakes or eggs and bacon each morning is because your culture tells you this is the proper thing to do. It is part of American culture. Food like this would be very strange to people growing up in other cultures. I remember walking up to a hotel breakfast buffet in China a few years ago and pausing with uncertainty. Should I try the cold duck eggs with a mysterious cold salad made of sprouts, or one of the doughy balls oozing something stringy that looked suspiciously like animal intestines? Or maybe a bowl of that watery porridge the locals were dipping up? While I was uneasily eyeing my options and trying to calm my churning stomach, the Chinese were perfectly at ease. They saw this selection of food as inviting as I see cornflakes or an omelet. When I had stepped off the airplane the day before, I wasn't just in a new country, I was in a new culture.

All of us are born into a particular set of cultural norms. We grow up watching how those around us respond in certain situations, how they dress, what they eat—and it subconsciously becomes normal. Our culture becomes the reference point by which we see life and judge what is right or wrong. Consequently, it is essential that we as believers look closely at our surrounding culture and its power to influence us.

Cultural Change

Cultures seem static, but they are always changing. Historically, there have been times when change was slow. Things continued relatively the same for many years, sometimes even centuries. You can still travel to places where Western influence and development have had little impact, and it is fascinating to see how little has changed from centuries ago. Their housing, food, and way of life seem untouched, while in more developed countries change has occurred quite rapidly.

Cultural change has a powerful impact on our lives, our view of "normal," how we think, and our perception of right and wrong. These changes also have a tremendous impact on our churches.

Consider how American culture has changed regarding the Biblical principle of modesty. In the early 1900s, women's swimsuits had high necks, long sleeves, and skirts or bloomers. Anything less modest was legally banned on many American beaches. Women were expected to be covered, and those who refused to abide by the law were treated as offenders. In 1908, film star Annette Kellerman was arrested at Revere Beach in Boston, Massachusetts, for wearing a one-piece bathing suit. In 1921, a bather in Atlantic City, New Jersey, was arrested for indecent exposure. Her crime? She was wearing her stockings rolled down, exposing her knees.[1]

How can a society's view of modesty change so rapidly? And more to the point, how has this affected conservative Christianity's view of modesty? Have we moved with the culture? Are we taking our readings from surrounding society? The answer for most of us, unfortunately, is yes. We have been impacted by surrounding culture.

Several years ago I flew across the country to give a seminar, and as we left the airport, the pastor who had picked me up began to share some of his congregation's struggles. As he talked, I marveled at how similar our issues were and what a huge influence the surrounding culture has on our congregations, regardless of where we live. He spoke of the constant battle they had over the size of the women's head covering. Many of their women were dissatisfied with the style of covering they had agreed upon as a church, and as we drove, he expressed his frustration. "Why is this a constant battle? Why can't our sisters just be content with the size and style of covering we have chosen?"

I have thought back to his question many times. Why were their sisters constantly making small alterations to their coverings? What a strange thing to keep messing with! The Biblical principle hasn't changed, so what has? The answer should be clear. The surrounding professing Christian culture has shifted, and this was affecting his congregation. While at one time most professing Christian women obeyed the command to be covered while praying, at least during services, now the covering has been explained away. Continuing to wear an outdated expression of submission carries with it a little embarrassment.

But consider for a moment a different setting. Imagine the evangelical world just waking up to the Scriptural command in 1 Corinthians 11. Books about covering women's heads are bestsellers and Christianity's most popular speakers are giving seminars on "The Exciting Relevance of the Women's Head Veiling." Local churches are encouraging their women to cover their heads, and the style many are embracing is larger than what your sisters are wearing. Wearing a veil is now trendy and speaks of vibrant Christianity!

If this was the surrounding Christian culture, would conservative churches still struggle with shrinking coverings?

Cultural Honesty

We aren't always honest about the impact of culture on our churches and lives. We have failed to acknowledge how fast societal mores are shifting and how this impacts our decisions. Almost every church, seminar, and book that professes to be Christian claims the Bible as its foundation. Approximately 20 percent of Americans (60 million) claim to be fundamental Christians, holding the Bible as inerrant.[2] Yet despite this religious claim, the vast majority live daily lives almost identical to American culture. They enjoy the same entertainment, have similar views on wealth, and divorce their spouses at about the same rate as the society with which they rub shoulders. Clearly, modern Christianity is being driven more by culture than by the teachings of Scripture. And as we read its books, observe its lives, and listen to its teachings, our view of what it means to follow Jesus tends to shift as well.

This can affect our view of issues on which the Bible is very clear. Our stance on topics like political involvement, the permanence of marriage, and sexual perversion can grow cloudy over time. We just aren't so sure anymore. This Christian culture influences family life, our values, and how we regard money and possessions. Many around us seem to be good Christians, and our view of what is normal can slowly shift. It is easy to say that what we do is based on the Bible, but we fail to realize that our lives are being shaped by other pressures as well.

I suggest there are three areas we need to be honest with regarding culture:

1. **We are moved by the "normal" around us.** Culture affects us in myriad ways. Some are tempted by fashion, fads, and ever-changing styles, while others develop an unhealthy counterculture perspective. They become so fearful of popular culture that doing things differently than society becomes the primary goal. Whatever our tendency, we need to honestly address it. Culture tends to move us.

2. **"Normal" is always changing.** Western culture has subjected us to unprecedented change. I think it is safe to say there has never been a time in history when so much cultural change has occurred in so short a time. Recently the French government tried to ban Muslim women from wearing modest swimsuits that cover almost all of their bodies. While the underlying reason for the French objection to wearing "burkinis" has more to do with religion than modesty, one can't help but be astounded at the cultural shift.

   In the early 1900s a woman could be arrested for not keeping her stockings above her knees. In 2016 a Muslim woman in Nice, France, was required to remove some of her clothes. The citation she received said she was not wearing "an outfit respecting good morals and secularism."[3] While this is an unusual situation due to concern about Muslim extremists and terrorism, it is hard to imagine a more drastic shift. Walking through a local grocery store today, we see people dressed in ways that were illegal less than a century ago. If your reference point is "normal," you will drift. Normal is always moving.

3. **The Bible must establish "normal."** It is vital to keep going back to the Word of God and ensure that this is actually our primary reference. It is easy to claim we are

using the Bible as our guide. Almost every Christian group out there is saying that. But is it actually our primary reference point? Every church tends to move over time, and it is tempting to count on church guidelines to arrest this drift. While some agreements are good and necessary, nothing but a constant focus on Scriptural principle will remind us how fast the "normal" of surrounding culture is moving.

Not too many years ago almost all visual entertainment came by way of the television. Consequently, churches could deal with this concern by deciding not to have a television in the home. But those days are gone. Today one can connect with the entertainment world in many ways and on many devices. A rule against television won't provide the same protection it once did.

Culture moves. If churches are going to survive and be effective, they will need to do more than develop more guidelines. They will also need to teach and discuss how these changes should be viewed in light of Biblical principle. Let the Word of God establish normalcy.

God has called us to be salt and light in our world, yet we often become so enamored with the surrounding society that we fail to shine. And when we become like the culture in which we are immersed, we fail to offer the beautiful alternative that God is calling us to exhibit. The call to remain separate from the world while reaching out to it creates tension in almost every church.

CHAPTER EIGHT

Culture: Examining Our Relationship

Every church relates to culture in some way. The question is, How are you as a church relating to culture? Are you intentionally addressing its impact from a Biblical perspective, or just comparing yourself with others and slowly drifting, always behind the culture at large, but still keeping pace?

Let's begin by looking at how Western churches tend to deal with culture, using the area of dress or personal appearance as an example. In the last chapter we looked at the dramatic move our society has made regarding modesty. Every church in America has been affected by this shift, but not all have dealt with it in the same way.

Dress

At the bottom of the chart on the next page is a continuum of change. On the left are groups that have focused on avoiding drift in dress. We call them non-assimilated groups, meaning they have strongly resisted assimilation into surrounding society. They have chosen to regulate and enforce how members of their churches dress. Consequently, they look very different from the culture around them.

To the right are groups that have chosen not to focus on clothing

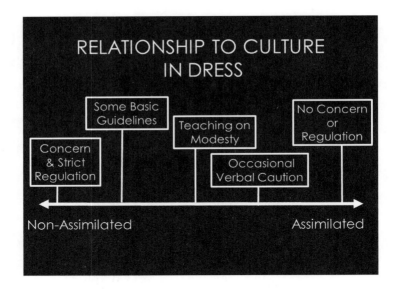

or personal appearance and have completely assimilated into society in this area. They dress like their neighbors and see little advantage in looking different. In between these two extremes are a variety of ways this cultural pressure is being addressed.

There may be good arguments for each of these positions, and our goal for now isn't to debate the best position. The question is, Can you identify where you are and why you are there?

Music

Let's look at another area in which we relate to culture. Few expressions of culture have changed as rapidly as music. Western society has been hit by an entertainment tsunami. From the Gregorian or monastic chants of the ancients to the rock and roll of the 1960s, the way people view music has completely changed. This cultural upheaval has had a dramatic effect on evangelical Christian worship as well. For hundreds of years believers chanted the Psalms in unison, and the primary focus was on the message contained in the words. Today, contemporary Christian music has made rhythm preeminent and tried to merge religious lyrics with secular music.

Churches have responded differently to this astounding change.

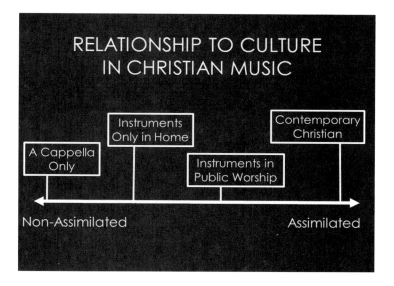

Those who have resisted cultural assimilation most strongly, shown on the far left of the continuum above, insist that no musical instruments be used. Those on the right side of the chart argue that godly words make a godly song, regardless of the tune or style of accompaniment.

Again, stop and consider your church's position. The point in this illustration is not whether your position is correct. Rather, are you taking cultural movement seriously? Can you identify your church's position on this continuum? Are you able to talk about the shift in music culture and its potential effect on your congregation? Or does this kind of discussion cause tension and conflict?

No matter what the topic, it is essential that congregations, and especially the leadership, be able to articulate why you have chosen to be where you are. Take any topic relating to culture and place it on the continuum. A good leader should be able to explain why your church has chosen not to be to the right or left of where you are. In fact, I suggest that a group's ability to explain and defend its position may be more important than the position they have chosen. Why? Because there is a strong tendency to move along this line.

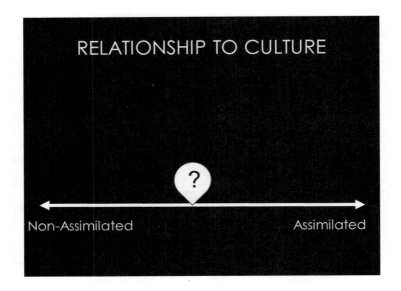

Look back at the diagrams showing potential positions regarding dress and music. Without a doubt, you can think of a church that has moved along these lines. Churches have had a very difficult time maintaining position. So why do churches move? Every church meets regularly, reads from the Bible, and listens to sermons. Most have a desire to apply Scriptural principles to everyday life. Further, I don't know of any church that doesn't claim to be basing beliefs on the Bible's teachings. So why the movement?

We need to acknowledge that sometimes change is a good thing. I can think of churches that realized their current path was moving away from Biblical principle, and they chose to change. But far too often there are other forces at work. I want to look at two other reasons churches tend to move, one direction or the other, along this line.

Toward What We Love

I remember working with a young man who spent a lot of time worrying about his looks. He belonged to a conservative group, but was always pushing the group's standards. Cool sunglasses, T-shirts, designer jeans—he seemed intent on following the fashions

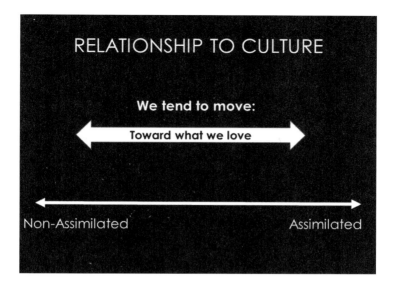

of surrounding society. Like some we saw in Neidmor Outreach's church, it was apparent that he loved the world's values and current fashion. Many people tried to work with him, but he slowly moved along this continuum toward the world, and today the transition is complete. Like Demas, he "loved this present world"[a] and walked away from Christianity. He finally arrived at the place he loved.

I can think of another individual with an opposite bent. He had been raised in a typical American home and became enamored with the "plain look." His conversations revolved around it. He debated with other members over which type of apparel was more conservative, and like Firmon Tradition's church, he slowly moved toward total non-assimilation. His church brothers were concerned. It seemed his love and devotion to a certain look was stronger than his desire for a relationship with Jesus Christ. Today, he has turned his back on both. Once he was as anti-culture as he could go, he found a lack of fulfillment and satisfaction.

We tend to move toward what we love. But there is another reason

---

[a] 2 Timothy 4:10

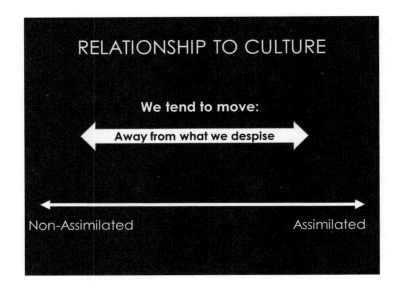

we move along this line. We tend to move away from what we despise. Let's go back to Neidmor Outreach and Firmon Tradition and take a closer look at the continued fallout that tends to follow church conflict and separation.

Away from What We Despise

When Firmon Tradition started his new fellowship, he was followed by a young man named Nathaniel Nitpick. Nathaniel loved to read church history, understood the danger of worldliness, and could explain just what happens when churches neglect the threat of acculturation. To Nathaniel Nitpick, Neidmor Outreach's church was a living example of slow drift toward the world, and he despised what he observed. He saw the bright colors and changing hairstyles, and to Nathaniel the solution was obvious. The safest place for a church was as far away from the world as possible. As Neidmor Outreach's church slowly drifted toward cultural assimilation, Nathaniel Nitpick moved in the opposite direction. Pastor Firmon was concerned as Nathaniel became more and more obsessed with rules and details. In the end there was little in Nathaniel Nitpick's life that would compel a seeker to inquire. He had continued moving further and further from what he despised and arrived at a place of cold legalism.

When Neidmor Outreach started his new fellowship, he was followed by a young man named Larry Looselove. Larry understood the foolishness of legalism, loved to speak of freedom in Christ, and was good at explaining why salvation will never be found in rules. To him, Firmon Tradition's church was a living example of what happens when a church focuses on rules instead of Christ. Larry shook his head each time Firmon's church got more detailed in their dress code, and nodded his head each time they experienced another internal conflict. To Larry the problem was obvious. Christianity is to be a growing love story, not a growing set of rules. As Firmon Tradition's church moved away from society, Larry Looselove moved in the opposite direction. Pastor Neidmor became concerned as Larry slowly became more and more like surrounding culture. Finally, there was little in Larry Looselove's life that would interest a seeker. He had moved further and further away from what he despised.

Nathaniel Nitpick and Larry Looselove both moved along this continuum, but in opposite directions. They both focused on the spiritual imperfections of others and slowly moved away from what they despised. Both were Bible readers, faithfully attended their churches, and claimed to be followers of Jesus. But despite their claims of being anchored in Biblical truth, their reference point was actually the church down the street. Both drifted because they were reacting to their past and being driven by the spiritual flaws of others. Nathaniel Nitpick and Larry Looselove's stories seem very different, yet there is something very similar. Both were more focused on where they had been than on where they were going.

> Both were more focused on where they had been than on where they were going.

Drifting or Anchored?

What about your church? Are you anchored or adrift? I have listened to many church leaders lament that their congregations seem to be moving. They try to admonish them occasionally or provide some good Biblical teaching on pertinent topics. But little by little, change happens. I have never met a pastor who enjoys spending his life addressing minor alterations in dress or other seemingly insignificant details.

But we must back up and look at root causes. We move toward what we love and away from what we despise. And when our reference point becomes our pain from the past, the church down the street, or anything other than the unchanging Word of God, drift is inevitable. I remember hearing a minister address the decisions we make in our relationship to culture. He was referring to a specific situation where he felt we were losing ground, and he asked, "Are we changing because of design or default?" In other words, are we intentionally deciding to make a change or just drifting along without thinking? If you are going to survive as a church, you will need to be purposeful as you relate to culture.

CHAPTER NINE

Culture: How Much Should We Embrace?

I still remember the first time I tried eating fufu in Ghana. This starchy paste made from cassava and green plantains is a staple food in many West African countries, and I didn't like it. I wanted to blend in with the Ghanaian people, to eat what they ate, and to show that even though my skin was a different color, I was like them. So I choked down the slimy fufu. On my next trip to Ghana, I inwardly chastised myself. *They enjoy this gooey mass; why can't I? Just think positively about fufu. After all, millions of people really like the stuff.* So when we ended up at the same restaurant, I again ordered fufu. Armed with my mental pep talk, I plowed into the jiggling blob. *Surely,* I reasoned, *it can't be as bad as I remembered.* It was.

One evening in Haiti after our work team had finished eating supper, we still had a large quantity of mashed potatoes and gravy. Knowing that many of the Haitian children milling around lacked calories, we offered our leftovers to them. They eagerly reached out and accepted our mashed potatoes and gravy, but I can still picture their reactions as they tasted it. They were trying to be polite, but their thoughts were clear. *You mean these Americans really like this slimy, mushy stuff? It just squishes in your mouth like mud and has the weirdest flavor.* In fact, the looks on their faces probably bore a strong resemblance to mine while eating fufu in Ghana!

"All Things to All Men"

Where you are born has a great impact on what food you enjoy. But if you are going to reach out to Ghanaian people, I would encourage you to learn to like fufu. (It is an acquired taste, and I am still in the learning process!) A Ghanaian will have a hard time relating with you when you don't enjoy, or even have any desire to enjoy, this part of his culture. The Apostle Paul told the Corinthians:

> And unto the Jews I became as a Jew, that I might gain the Jews; to them that are under the law, as under the law, that I might gain them that are under the law; to them that are without law, as without law, (being not without law to God, but under the law to Christ,) that I might gain them that are without law. To the weak became I as weak, that I might gain the weak: I am made all things to all men, that I might by all means save some. And this I do for the gospel's sake, that I might be partaker thereof with you.[a]

Notice those words, "I am made all things to all men, that I might by all means save some." Paul was willing to live differently in different settings in his attempt to reach out with the Gospel. He attempted to embrace local culture so men could better relate to him. I believe if Paul lived in Ghana, he would eat fufu. If we are going to reach out to the lost, we will need to consider this reality: we learn best from

---

[a] 1 Corinthians 9:20–23

those who resemble us and understand our culture. Paul was saying, "I am willing to do whatever it takes to reach out!" This is extremely important, even if it means eating fufu. After all, the type of food we eat is not very important from an eternal perspective. Paul knew that if the believers at Corinth were going to reach out to the people around them, they needed to have some commonality.

Come Out and Be Separate
Turn just a few pages in your Bible and Paul says something that sounds entirely different. The city of Corinth was known for ungodliness, and Paul issued this strong warning:

> Be ye not unequally yoked together with unbelievers: for what fellowship hath righteousness with unrighteousness? and what communion hath light with darkness? And what concord hath Christ with Belial? or what part hath he that believeth with an infidel? And what agreement hath the temple of God with idols? for ye are the temple of the living God; as God hath said, I will dwell in them, and walk in them; and I will be their God, and they shall be my people. Wherefore come out from among them, and be ye separate, saith the Lord, and touch not the unclean thing; and I will receive you, and will be a Father unto you, and ye shall be my sons and daughters, saith the Lord Almighty.[b]

Paul was reminding them that the ungodly Corinthian culture was headed downhill. If this church was going to thrive, its members needed to separate themselves from that influence. He also told the church at Rome to "be not conformed to this world."[c] Paul was aware that for the believers to survive, they must come out from surrounding culture and be separate.

---

[b] 2 Corinthians 6:14–18
[c] Romans 12:2

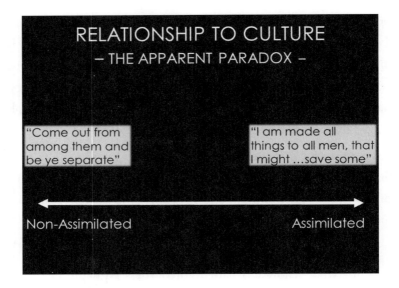

The Apparent Paradox

We are obviously called to love our neighbor while maintaining separation from the world, but too often a tension develops between these two positions. How should a church respond to this apparent paradox shown on this chart?

Before you embrace one of these positions and esteem it to be more important than the other, consider this: there is danger at both ends. Churches like Neidmor Outreach's that keep creeping down the line toward assimilation will eventually become so like the world they will be of little value in reaching out. As Rod Dreher, author of *The Benedict Option,* said, "A church that looks and talks and sounds just like the world has no reason to exist."[1] When our lifestyles, use of entertainment, and how we present ourselves in public are just like the world's, we will no longer be effective in calling people higher. We become irrelevant in our efforts to reach out.

On the other end of the spectrum, churches like Firmon Tradition's will focus on being different and will slowly creep down the line toward being non-assimilated. Eventually they become irrelevant as well. When you become so different that your fellow man feels

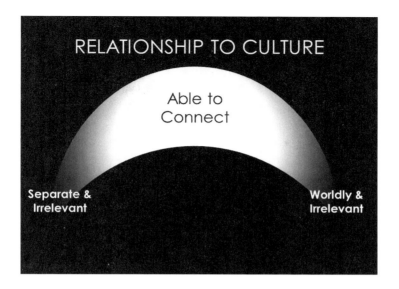

you do not understand his struggles, it is difficult to build a meaningful relationship. On the one end is "sanctified" laziness—separating ourselves from the lost, enjoying and finding our fulfillment in being with family and others who are like us. On the other end is pious worldliness—chasing after all the pleasures our culture has to offer, all the while justifying our pursuit by saying we need to be like them to save them. One author said it like this: "If there is no accommodation [to culture], Christianity is unintelligible and cannot spread; if there is too much accommodation, it will spread, but will no longer be Christianity."[2]

How Much Culture Should We Accommodate?

All of us accept some culture. The food we eat, the colors we prefer, our methods of transportation, and the style of house we live in—our culture affects these choices. Some choices do not really matter. Most of us can agree that there is little danger in eating the same food as our surrounding culture. Even the most counterculture groups in America enjoy a good hamburger. But other choices are not as clear. What about fashions and styles that keep changing? Firmon

Tradition's church would argue that followers of Jesus should purposely appear different in public. They should make it clear they are not of this world.

Neidmor Outreach's church would see this differently. They would argue that a few changes in dress would make them more seeker-friendly. However, if a church decides to look a little more like surrounding society, just how much ground should be given? Where is the line between being able to connect with neighbors and being worldly and therefore ineffective?

Tanya Trendy is a faithful member of her church. She looks forward to prayer meetings, and you can always count on her presence at Bible study. She is enthusiastic about serving the Lord, and everyone enjoys her friendliness and exuberant personality. Tanya works in the local grocery store and is concerned about the souls of her unbelieving coworkers, so she tries to build relationships with them. Sometimes she hangs out with them at Pizza Hut after hours, and other times they meet at the mall. Occasionally one of Tanya's friends comes to church with her.

Over time, however, her parents and church leaders become concerned about changes they are seeing in Tanya. They seem hardly worth mentioning—small changes in appearance, use of popular slang, and subtle criticism of older members in the church. Tanya also seems unable to hold a face-to-face conversation without being interrupted by social media. She likes to watch an occasional movie because she finds this helpful in relating to the lives of her unconverted friends.

What is happening?

Tanya is being adversely impacted by culture. Regardless of our stated goal, when we primarily associate with those who have different values, subject ourselves to the oversaturation of advertising in shopping malls, and entertain ourselves with culture's media, we will change. Society's heroes become ours, and gradually a girl like Tanya will find herself admiring celebrities more than her pastor's wife.

We follow our heroes. Whether a young man secretly admires sports figures, a father admires wealthy businessmen, or a young girl like Tanya begins to admire the women on display in the mall, these cultural influences are very real and powerful. It is easy to make little accommodations, using relevance to our society as rationale, and find ourselves following a slippery slope toward worldliness and evangelistic irrelevance. So how can we avoid falling into this ditch?

Keeping God's Perspective

The easy answer is to ensure that our primary focus and reference is the Word of God. But how can we be sure this is the case? If you would ask Tanya Trendy, she would undoubtedly reply that her allegiance to the Word of God outweighs her love for culture. But we are not always good at discerning our own allegiance, and this is one of the reasons God has placed us in church families.

Remember, it is God's desire that every person be saved,[d] and He has called each of us to join Him in this work of reconciliation.[e] It is easy to become obsessed by the influence of culture and mentally overwhelmed by the power of darkness, forgetting that God is greater than these. We are called not only to protect what we have, but also to reach out to the lost. Our churches need to spend time collectively praying and discussing how we can best shine in a darkening world, yet this will require more than just discussion. If we are serious about reaching into a dark culture, we will also need to prayerfully set some boundaries for our brotherhoods.

Church rules or agreements have fallen out of favor in many churches. We want to teach principles without insisting on compliance to a list of rules. But perhaps much of our problem is that we have not looked at agreements through the lens of God's desire to evangelize. In his little booklet *Are Written Standards for the Church?* author John Coblentz says this:

---

[d] 1 Timothy 2:4, 2 Peter 3:9
[e] 1 Corinthians 3:9, 2 Corinthians 5:18–6:1

Where the church loses sight of its earthly mission to win the lost and disciple them for Jesus, internal fighting over standards and personalities and issues is almost inevitable. It is my belief that much of the controversy today over standards is related directly to a loss of evangelistic zeal. People who give themselves to winning the lost for Jesus have a basis for seeing issues in heaven's perspective. They weigh what they do, what they wear, and where they go in light of how it will affect their testimony both within the brotherhood and without. They view the things of this life against the realities of the next life. They make decisions about such things as hairstyles and worldly entertainment, for example, with a view to eternity.³

When our goal is primarily defensive preservation, our tendency will be to argue about details and the importance of self-focused and self-serving rules. Our attention is on ourselves. But when our focus includes the lost, quibbling about little things seems foolish, and submitting for the larger good becomes clearly vital for our vision.

Unashamed and Unapologetic
Recently I visited an inner-city mission here in America. The families I met had a passion for the lost, and I was impressed by their love for the outcasts of society. These families could have chosen to live down a long lane in the country, drinking iced tea on the porch and enjoying a comfortable middle-class lifestyle. Instead, they frequently see violence up close and have their schedules disrupted on a regular basis. An unexpected visitor in the middle of the night might turn out to be an eight-year-old neighbor child who is fearful of getting caught in the fighting between drunk parents and needs a safe place to sleep. I greatly admire their zeal and compassion for these hurting people.

But I observed something else. Although part of a conservative group, their young men's dress portrayed the "cool" look.

Everything—from hairstyle and faded jeans to T-shirts proclaiming secular messages—was trying to relate to local culture, trying to fit in. Young women's hairstyles, colorful scarves, and choice of dress material demonstrated their desire to avoid looking too "different." They knew they needed to be somewhat like surrounding culture to relate, and I believe this is what they were trying to do.

Even with all this effort, these families spoke of their frustration at not making a more significant impact in their neighborhood. They are trying to reach out and bless the community, but so far no locals have joined their fellowship. This certainly is not due to a lack of interest in religion. On the contrary, many in their neighborhood are experiencing significant spiritual transformation—to Islam! Walking around this community you can see many women wearing long-sleeved dresses and full Muslim *hijab*.[f] These are not ethnic Muslims or immigrants who brought their religious convictions with them; these are inner-city Americans who are making a deliberate choice.[4]

While there are many issues here, one fact seems obvious. People

---

[f] Full head and neck wrap

in this neighborhood are not avoiding converting to Christianity due to fear of looking weird. These new converts to Islam are dressing much more differently from inner-city culture than this conservative Christian church would ever require. Maybe these inner-city dwellers were not seeing these Christians as people in strange dress, but as people who are apologetic about who they are—people who are ashamed of their own culture and heritage. And if these Christians don't really believe in their culture, why would anyone in the neighborhood want what they have?

So what do we do with this? If we are going to relate to people, we will need to be somewhat like them. They will need to know that we understand their concerns, needs, and culture. Yet if we are going to avoid being absorbed by their entertainment and fashions, we will need to prayerfully make some choices that make us different. These choices must use Biblical principle as a reference point, and we must believe in God's culture as we embrace it. If we are apologetic about our heritage, our lifestyle, or our dress, we will not present the Gospel in a very compelling manner.

Where Are You?

Before moving on, think about your own life and congregation. Do you have a collective vision for reaching out, not just across the ocean, but in your own neighborhood? Are you able to openly discuss culture, or are you apologetic about being different from the world?

Satan can cause a church to become ineffective either by not addressing cultural pressures and slowly becoming assimilated into society, or by focusing on being different from our culture and forgetting the hurting people all around us who need the Lord Jesus. The first has little to offer a drifting society, while the second has little focus outside of themselves. Satan is pleased with either extreme. But in the next chapter we will look at an even more alarming tendency.

CHAPTER TEN

Finding Moderation Without Compromise

An even more deadly tendency than the two we just reviewed is assuming that a New Testament church vision should be right between those two—a little love for our neighbor and a little separation from the world. Let's go back and imagine what this error might look like in Firmon Tradition's and Neidmor Outreach's congregations.

Years have gone by now, and as Firmon Tradition looks around at his congregation, he is concerned. His members are aware of the New Testament teachings regarding separation from the world, but as time goes by, they seem to have less and less interest in their neighbors. He knows what the Bible says about loving our neighbors, so at their next leadership meeting he suggests they get involved in a prison ministry. There's not a lot of excitement about this, but after some discussion they agree. Firmon now feels satisfied. They aren't moving toward the world, and they now have a little outward focus as well.

Neidmor Outreach looks around at his congregation and is concerned as well. His congregation is cognizant of the New Testament teaching on loving our neighbors, but as time passes, they seem to be drifting toward the world. He knows what the Bible says about separation from the world, so at the next leadership meeting he suggests they set a few guidelines on outward appearance. There's not much enthusiasm about this suggestion, but the rules will not affect their lives too much, so eventually they agree. Neidmor is content. They are still involved in the lives of their neighbors, and now they also have some separation from the world.

Moderation and Compromise

Moderation is a Biblical principle,[a] and as you consider the above two scenarios, maybe moderation is what you see. But I suggest that these pastors are making compromises, not being moderate. Compromise is giving up one's principles, capitulating to less than the best. The two can sound so similar, but they are actually very different. The challenging truth is that moderation can be the Scriptural principle we hide behind, while in fact we are compromising Biblical truth.

Consider the life of Jesus. The Bible says that grace and truth came by Jesus Christ.[b] What did that look like in His life? Truth demands justice for sin, while grace provides mercy. It seems that these two are at opposite ends of a continuum. So how did Jesus accomplish this? Consider the chart on the right. Which way do you visualize the life of Christ?

Do you think Jesus was halfway truthful and just partly full of

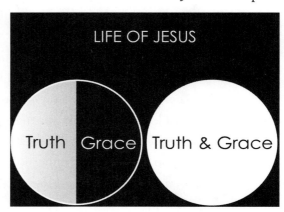

---

[a] Philippians 4:5
[b] John 1:17

grace? Of course not. Choosing to be partly truthful would have compromised His character, nature, and mission. And what about grace? Do you think Jesus added a little grace to His life to offset the harshness of justice and truth? No, He was all grace as well. Consequently, those who walked with Him every day and observed His life could report, "And the Word was made flesh, and dwelt among us, (and we beheld his glory, the glory as of the only begotten of the Father,) *full of grace and truth*"[c] (emphasis added). Anything else would have been compromise.

New Testament Church

This same principle applies to the church. It is easy to visualize the New Testament church a little like the chart below. We know we are to be separate, and we are aware that God has a deep concern for the lost. So we decide that the church should have a little of both. But consider the Apostle Paul. Do you

think he had a *little* interest in separating himself from the pull of surrounding society, and a *little* desire to reach the unbelievers he met? How absurd! In the third chapter of Philippians, Paul describes his culture's value system. He makes a list of all the things which were of great importance in his society, and which had at one time been of great value to him. But he concludes by denouncing this cultural value system, comparing the world's values to manure. That is not a half-hearted renunciation of the world!

---

[c] John 1:14

He was just as passionate in his desire that all men would be saved. As I look at his life, I see a man who daily poured himself into the lives of others, attempting to lead them to Christ. "Knowing therefore the terror of the Lord," he told the church at Corinth, "we persuade men."[d] He even went so far as to say he could wish himself accursed from Christ so that his Jewish brother could be saved.[e]

The Apostle Paul was sold out for Christ, dedicated to total separation from the world, yet totally committed to reaching out to the lost. To neglect either would have been compromising God's call on his life.

Our churches need to apply this same principle. We are not called to have a little separation from the world and a little interest in the lost. A New Testament church will have a strong passion for both.

A Little of This and a Little of That

A New Testament church will have a strong inner focus and a strong outer focus. It will not concentrate on one and then have a little of the other to keep it balanced. The result of that path is lukewarmness. This is not the picture we see in the book of

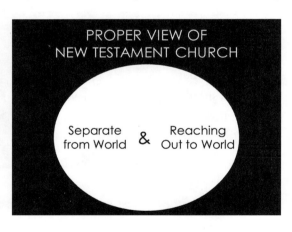

Acts, or in Revelation, where we get a vivid image of God's disgust for lukewarm believers.[f] We must come to see both separation and outreach as Scriptural and essential. The beautiful truth is that they actually complement each other. Our churches desperately need converted seekers from outside our circles. Those who have not been

---

[d] 2 Corinthians 5:11
[e] Romans 9:3
[f] Revelation 3:16

raised within a sheltered environment have an uncanny ability to spot hypocrisy. They can be very good at applying Scriptural truth to duplicity in our lives. In short, they can help us become much more consistent in our separation from the world.

Preserving and Promulgating

A truth that is worth preserving is also worth promulgating. This is a reality that Firmon Tradition needs to come to grips with. He believes his church has a proper grasp on the Gospel, has learned much from history, and knows that these truths need to be preserved. He is correct. But a truth valuable enough to be preserved

> A truth valuable enough to be preserved should also be shared.

should also be shared. The converse is also true. A truth worth promulgating is also worth preserving, a fact that Neidmor Outreach needs to learn. He believes that his church has the truth of Jesus Christ and it would be a sin not to share it with his neighbors. Neidmor needs to take a closer look at church history and at the end result of churches that have failed to adequately address cultural pressures. Firmon should go back to the book of Acts and examine what God wants the local church to be doing.

> A truth worth promulgating is also worth preserving.

Looking Within

Before leaving this section on the church and culture, we must address the impact that affluence and technology are having on our lives and churches.

I work in countries where the culture moves very slowly. Tools, housing, dress, and other visible areas seem hardly to change over centuries. Technology is starting to affect this, but in many settings there has been little change. As a result, they have not had to give much thought to the dangers of cultural change. We travel there, see their vibrant churches, and it is easy to conclude that since believers in these countries have a thriving faith with few boundaries on culture's inroads, we must not need them either. If they can do it, so can we.

However, we don't live there. We live in the midst of unprecedented cultural change. Technology constantly displays an amazing array of possibilities, and affluence allows us to pursue them. Churches that do not address this cultural drift are in great danger. With good reason the Apostle John gave the church a strong warning against loving the world,[g] and churches that are going to survive will need some counterculture agreements. But don't stop there.

> Develop a vision of a counterculture church that is actively reaching out to the world!

After you have prayerfully considered culture and taken steps to mitigate its danger, reach out to your neighbor. Have a concern for others and start building relationships with people. Develop a vision of a counterculture church that is actively reaching out to the world!

It is easy to believe that people won't listen to our message if we are not chasing the same fashions, but seekers will overlook differences in appearance if they feel genuinely loved. So go out and love people. Instead of building false virtual relationships with movie stars, sports figures, and the rich and famous on electronic media, develop real relationships with real people. Instead of retreating into little safe cocoons, reach out to hurting neighbors. If you approach them with a genuine love, God will reach them in ways you cannot even imagine!

---

[g] 1 John 2:15

PART THREE

BUSINESS and BROTHERHOOD:
Rethinking the Relationship

CHAPTER ELEVEN

Business and Brotherhood: The Problem

When considering church vision and ways of building relationships with people, our occupations are an important yet often overlooked element. Stop for a moment and consider your neighbors. If someone went door to door and asked what people thought about the members of your church, what would they say? I am sure they would have opinions, but how were they formed?

Have they examined your statement of faith or your doctrinal beliefs and compared them to the Bible? Probably not. In fact, I suggest that most of your neighbors have given little thought to your stated beliefs. Rather, they have drawn conclusions based on their frequent interactions with your members. They have watched the choices you make, how you relate to others in the community, and how you respond to difficult situations. I would propose that many of these interactions occur in the marketplace, which is why occupational interactions must be considered when developing a church vision.

After writing the rough draft of the book *It's Not Your Business,* I sent the manuscript to various reviewers for input. This is a normal process, a safeguard against publishing something with unsound doctrine or faulty logic. But I always have a bit of trepidation as these reports return. One of them in particular caught my attention. It was from a reviewer I consider a brother, mentor, and friend, and I highly respect his opinion. So I took his comments and concern regarding this book on Christian business seriously. Here is what he wrote:

> Despite Gary's compelling rationale for the development of Christian business, I am left with one nagging question. Considering that businesses seem more often than not to be a snare to their owners and developers, should we give this much encouragement to business development?

In other words, given all the spiritual problems businesses create in the owners' lives and in our churches, should we really encourage men to pursue business? He explained further.

> Of course, I was particularly blessed by the ideal of a business that "shows what the whole world of commerce would be like if everybody obeyed the King." This articulates the very heart of a kingdom of God perspective, and it would be great if this could happen. But how likely is this to happen in the Christian business world given the tendency of wholesale capitulation to self-centered financial pursuit echoed repeatedly in this book? Will not the discussion tend to encourage business involvement more than it deters Christians from the traditional pursuit of wealth for selfish ends?

The book had not been printed yet, and I remember lying awake wrestling with his comments. Was it possible that the message in this book would ultimately be a spiritual curse in the lives of my brothers?

Business and wealth have indeed been a challenge for the church in America. We don't seem to be as good at stewarding our finances as we like to think. In addition to the problems associated with the wealth business creates, many businessmen have been distracted by business itself. Jesus clearly warned about these distractions. In His parable of the sower, the seed that fell among thorns represented individuals who became distracted by earthly things. "And the cares of this world, and the deceitfulness of riches, and the lusts of other things entering in, choke the word, and it becometh unfruitful."[a]

In this passage Jesus gives several distractions that can make us unfruitful, and I suggest that involvement in business increases this likelihood. First there are the cares of this world. This includes all the daily decisions and accompanying stress that go with keeping an enterprise afloat. Then there is the deceitfulness of riches. This temptation does not just affect those who are successful. The belief that wealth is the answer to life's problems can take hold in those who are poor as well. Paul told Timothy it is those who "will be rich"[b] who are tempted and ensnared. However, anyone who is successful financially will face a strong temptation to lean on his wealth. Finally, Jesus warns us about the lusts of other things—getting distracted by the cares of life, business activities, and the many things money can buy. All of this has powerfully affected the spiritual lives of business owners and left a tremendous impact on our churches. Our businesses have affected our brotherhoods.

Let's take a closer look at ways men become distracted by business.

The Diverting of Gifts

God has distributed some remarkable abilities in the body of Christ, and one of these is the gift of administration. Successful businessmen can examine a problem, pinpoint the root cause, and provide a workable solution. There is great need within the body of Christ for

---

[a] Mark 4:19
[b] 1 Timothy 6:9

this gift. Think about this as you read through Paul's list of qualifications for bishops and deacons in his letter to Timothy.[c] Timothy was to be looking for men like this, men of integrity who could rule well. But there is an interesting corollary here. Some of the same gifts that make a man valuable within the brotherhood can also make him very successful in business. This does not mean that a man who knows how to make money will automatically be a good leader in the church. But diligence, energy, focus, and the capability to teach and administer are very useful gifts in both business and the brotherhood. The challenge is to keep men with these gifts focused on the kingdom of God.

> Some of the same gifts that make a man valuable within the brotherhood can also make him very successful in business.

I have watched men, obviously gifted by God, become ensnared by business. I believe there are several reasons this occurs. Perhaps they haven't been called to positions of leadership within the church, and their unused energy gets poured into their businesses. In a healthy capitalistic environment this often translates into business success and financial wealth. Or maybe they have been called into church leadership, but they find their occupations more fulfilling than shepherding an unruly flock. In business we can measure success by growth on the balance sheet. But how can a man ever "succeed" in church life? Dealing with one difficult relationship after another is wearying, and it becomes easy to shift attention to business.

In either situation, business has diverted the man's attention. Instead of pouring his primary focus and energy into the kingdom of God, he finds himself drawing his daily satisfaction from his

---

[c] 1 Timothy 3:1–13

business. Occupations play a part in building the kingdom of God, but they were never intended to be our source of fulfillment and life.

The Diverting of Wealth

While finances are needed in a community, wealth has rarely been positive within brotherhoods. After the persecution of the Anabaptists during the Reformation in the 1500s came a time of great prosperity. Many descendants of the martyrs became prosperous. The same steadfastness and zeal that had helped their forefathers endure great torture was now turned toward commerce. Just one hundred years after major persecution, the writer of *Martyrs Mirror* lamented, "These are sad times, in which we live; nay, truly, there is more danger now than in the time of our fathers who suffered death for the testimony of the Lord."

This is an astonishing statement from someone who was enjoying prosperity. He goes on to describe the observations that troubled him.

> Hence arises that shameful and vast commerce which extends far beyond the sea into other parts of the world, but which notwithstanding cannot satisfy those who love it. . . . Numerous large, expensive and ornamented houses, country-seats of splendid architecture and provided with towers, parks magnificent as a paradise and other embellished pleasure-grounds, which are seen on every hand. . . . Great dinners, lavish banquets and wedding feasts . . .[1]

This was a time when many people still lived in poverty. The author mourned the fact that his people were ignoring the poor. Funds that should have been going to them were being "squandered and consumed."[2] Unfortunately, the church's tendency has been to shine during times of persecution, then selfishly consume the resources God provides during times of prosperity. There have been exceptions, but the church's track record during affluence hasn't been good. And wealth has created still another problem in our brotherhoods.

"Some Are More Equal Than Others"

In 1946 George Orwell produced a small controversial book titled *Animal Farm*.³ It was written at a time when England and Russia had a wartime alliance, and Orwell was concerned about the high regard the British had for Joseph Stalin, the communist dictator of Russia. *Animal Farm* is an allegory in which animals take over a British farm and set up an animal commune where everything is shared equally. All the animals were to be on equal footing; the mantra they all recited was, "All animals are equal." Different animals had various roles or tasks, but none was greater than another. Eventually the pigs, who were the brains of the outfit, began to take little liberties. Since they were the thinkers, it seemed logical to them that they should have the best food and do the least manual labor. The pigs represented communist Russian leadership, and Orwell's goal was to show that absolute power, regardless of how lofty the intentions, would ultimately corrupt.

As the pigs assumed more privileges and did less work, events rose to a climax. The pigs were in the farmhouse all day, clearly getting fatter from doing no work, while the other animals were nearing starvation. To explain this disparity, the pigs offered an explanation to the less fortunate and down-trodden animals, a saying which has since become famous: "All animals are equal, but some are more equal than others."

As I have listened to people share about the difficulties surrounding the relationship between business and brotherhood, I am reminded of this quote. Almost every Bible-believing church claims that everyone is on the same level. Some may have different roles or be given different tasks, but no one is higher than anyone else. Like the animals chanting in Orwell's book, we like to frequently repeat this refrain. But is it true? What about the man who is known to have more money than the rest of the members? Does the man known for his business acumen subtly become "more equal" than others? Does a brother's ability in business impact his perceived value in the body of Christ?

The Golden Rule

The Bible speaks of this tendency to honor those who have wealth. James calls it respect of persons and tells us it is sin.[d] Yet we struggle with this. When a man is good in business, has wealth, and employs a good portion of a congregation, he often has disproportionate influence. At times this is referred to as the golden rule: "Whoever has the gold makes the rules." This can be a real challenge for congregations. Businessmen, especially in isolated areas, provide vital employment. Young families often depend on local enterprises for survival. Yet if the overall impact is to be positive, the owners of these businesses will need to operate in humility, and the church must carefully hold these men accountable.

On the other hand, many brotherhoods don't recognize the blessing of business. A certain natural tension exists between employer and employee, and seldom do employees view their bosses with great admiration. It does happen, but it is rare. As a result, a congregation may have a good businessman who provides them with jobs and income, yet people might disdain that blessing. Businessmen tend to be either exalted or despised.

> Businessmen tend to be either exalted or despised.

Your Church?

How a successful businessman uses his income and business has a tremendous impact on how he will be regarded by his brotherhood. If he uses his financial resources primarily for himself, he may never understand

---

[d] James 2:1–9

why he's not appreciated. But if he faithfully uses the abilities God has given him, provides jobs for others, lives simply, and demonstrates Jesus Christ in the marketplace, his fellow members will be much more likely to value his gift.

Is there tension in your church between businesses and the brotherhood? Are some more equal than others? Of course we would never say this. We like to promote the thought that we are on one level. We are all saved by the blood of Jesus, and it is only His presence and power in our lives that gives us worth. That is what we profess, but in reality, is everyone viewed the same? Or have we allowed our views of wealth and business—temporal things with no eternal value—to cause us to view blood-bought saints differently?

CHAPTER TWELVE

Is Business a Blessing?

Looking out over the Mountain Meadows congregation on a Sunday morning, a newcomer would see little difference between the men. They are all well-dressed and friendly, just as you would expect to find in the average conservative Christian church. But if you sat in the pews every Sunday, one of the men would stand out. You might or might not admire him, but you would have to admit that something is different about Simon Sharp.

Simon is the owner of Sharp Storage Sheds, a large company that employs almost half the men in the Mountain Meadows congregation. In addition, Simon is involved in local land development. He is well known in the community and owns numerous rental properties. In fact, several families in the congregation rent Simon's houses. But all a visitor would observe is that Simon, one of the ministers, is an outgoing leader. When there is a perplexing question, Simon puts things in perspective and formulates a logical answer. He is well-read and can quickly point to Bible passages that address the issue at hand. When preaching, he comforts the sorrowful, tells stories for the children, and points the sinner to Jesus Christ. Simon frequently encourages his church to be more active in evangelism. It was his idea to put a rack of tracts in the foyer, and he frequently encourages his congregation to pass out literature to neighbors and coworkers.

Mountain Meadows Musings

Simon Sharp is an integral part of his local congregation. Not only do the members look to him as a spiritual leader, they also depend upon his generosity for financial needs. The members of Mountain Meadows know their private school would not exist without his liberal contributions. Of course, all donations are anonymous, but when large sums are deposited in the local bank, everyone knows where they came from. Simon is also generous with employment opportunities. Not only do many of the men receive their paychecks from Sharp Storage Sheds, but it has also become a wonderful place for the young men to learn basic skills and develop a good work ethic. Not every member may agree with all of Simon Sharp's personal financial decisions, and some might even have concerns about his focus on business success; yet most would agree that God has blessed Simon's business, and it has blessed their congregation in multiple ways.

However, if you could go out into the community or even enter his shop and listen to a few of the discussions, you would hear other perspectives. Let's listen in on some conversations.

In the Shed Shop

Setting down his lunchbox, Charley leaned against the wall with a sigh. "Sounds like the boss is off to Hawaii again. Tough life!"

George munched on his sandwich. "Wonder what that would be like? Walking along the beach, palm trees waving, listening to the waves and seagulls. I wouldn't mind trying it for a week."

"Forget it, George. It isn't gonna happen. Look at Tim. He manages the shop and works harder than anyone else, but he obviously won't be going to Hawaii anytime soon. With eight children, hospital bills from his wife's surgery, and that mortgage payment coming every month, I don't see him sitting on a beach for a long while. If Tim can't make it to Hawaii, you and I can kiss that dream goodbye!"

George peered back into his lunchbox and pulled out an apple. "Yeah. In many ways Simon's and Tim's lives are the same. They have desks in the same office, they both work hard every day, and they even go to the same church. Yet one of them struggles to pay his bills and the other one is on the beach!"

"Yeah. Kind of strange too. If I had a second home like Simon's up there in the mountains, I don't think I'd worry about Hawaii."

At the Lumberyard

Slamming down the phone, the secretary sighed and rubbed her forehead. "Sharp Storage Sheds again, complaining about that last load. There were several crooked pieces inside one of the piles."

Jack, the owner, looked up and rolled his eyes. "And let me guess. It was Shrewd Simon himself trying to get another 10 percent off because two pieces were slightly crooked."

"Close, but this time it was 15 percent off. He said if we don't cut the price, he may have to start looking around for another supplier."

"We can't cut the price any further. This is getting ridiculous! Last time there were three studs that had some bark on them, and he wanted 10 percent off the entire load. I don't know what to do with that miser! We do the best we can, and he still complains. I hate to lose him as a customer, but he's almost impossible to work with."

The bookkeeper chimed in from across the room. "It would sure make bookkeeping easier without him! Almost every month I have to call to get paid. And even though Simon pays late, he wants the discount for paying early!"

At the Attorney's Office

"Jim, don't forget. You have an appointment at 9:00 with Simon Sharp."

"Thanks, Sally. How could I forget? Sometimes I think his name should be Simon Sly. I always look forward to his visits. I have never seen anyone so adept at applying pressure without using force. It sure makes my job interesting!"

Sally propped her chin on her hand. "He has always confused me. From the outside his church looks very simple, open, and transparent—almost like the best of the olden days when people were honest and straightforward. Yet Simon's business life seems so complex."

Jim looked up. "What do you mean?"

"Well, like that family down on Third Street that Simon wanted to evict. Most landlords would have filed the papers, forced the family to get out, and moved on. But Simon goes through all these maneuvers, keeping his name off all the court orders, and in the end the only name on the papers was a property management company. Why pay someone else and go through all that when Simon could have easily done it himself?"

"It's not very complicated, Sally. His church has a rule against using the courts, so that forces him to hire someone else to do it. I've been involved in many similar projects. This thing of not using the legal system is just a smoke screen. When it comes right down to it, they evict and use collection agencies like everyone else. They just have some church rules they need to work around. Nice folks, but peel back the façade, and they're not much different from anyone else."

Simon Sharp

So, is Simon Sharp's business a blessing to the Mountain Meadows congregation? The answer will depend largely on what the church is trying to achieve. There are some obvious blessings. Simon's business is providing income for families, allowing young men to develop a strong work ethic, and providing revenue that allows Mountain Meadows' private school to function. If their purpose is to have a nice place to raise families, a good school for their children, and a way to develop and pass on a good work ethic, we would have to say Simon is instrumental in helping them achieve those goals.

But what if Mountain Meadows wants more? Let's assume their vision also includes reaching out to the community with the message of Jesus and demonstrating the kingdom of God in every aspect of their lives. Are Simon's business and financial dealings helping the congregation achieve this goal?

CHAPTER THIRTEEN

Business: Understanding the Potential

Just south of Athens, Greece, in the city of Epidaurus, is a large theater that has baffled researchers and historians. Built several centuries before the time of Christ, this huge structure must have taken many years to construct. Yet the primary attraction for researchers and tourists is not the amphitheater's size, but its extraordinary acoustics. A speaker standing in the center of the open-air stage can be heard clearly in the back rows two hundred feet away. Architects and archaeologists have speculated for years on what makes sound transmit so well in this amphitheater.

Some have argued that this phenomenon is primarily due to the use of porous limestone risers, which suppress low-frequency sound. Others argue that it is simply the design and shape of the structure. Still others contend that wind blowing from the stage to the audience is one of the primary factors. Whatever the cause, the effect is striking. An audience of 14,000 can clearly hear a performer on the stage with no amplification, without the actor even raising his voice.

Audiophiles, or enthusiasts of high quality sound, refer to certain places in a room as "sweet spots." A sweet spot is a location where a combination of factors results in the greatest listening pleasure. Years ago I worked for a man who spent hours finding the perfect place in his house to listen to music. When he found the precise location where his ears could receive the perfect blend of music from multiple speakers, he placed his recliner there and put tape on the floor around it so he wouldn't lose the spot. That was the sweet spot. This same principle applies to where a speaker or actor stands. Many stages have a sweet spot—a place from which an actor will best be heard by the audience.

If you visit the theatre of Epidaurus, you will find a flat stone in the center of the stage. When

actors perform, they try to stay as close as possible to this stone. It is the sweet spot. Buses carrying throngs of curious tourists roll in, and tour guides ask the group to sit high up on the stone seats while the guide stands on the stone and talks in a normal voice. Tourists sitting two hundred feet away marvel at how clearly they can hear.

A Neglected Sweet Spot

I suggest that our daily occupational lives are a neglected sweet spot for evangelism. Our businesses provide a beautiful place, a stage if you will, to proclaim the Gospel. It is a place where the music that our churches should be producing can be played and heard by an entire community. It might be a retail store known for ensuring that each customer is pleased, an appliance repair shop known for providing more than people expect, or a diligent young man who always arrives early and exceeds his boss's expectations. When believers apply Biblical principles in their daily occupations, it provides a tremendous platform for kingdom expansion.

> Great stages don't necessarily guarantee great music.

However, great stages don't necessarily guarantee great music. Our occupations, which can be incredible stages for the Gospel, can also destroy the message and do incredible damage.

Destructive Potential

In the last chapter we looked at Simon Sharp, a church leader whose desire to reach out to his neighbors was exemplified by providing gospel tracts and encouraging his congregation to distribute them regularly. But just how compelling would a gospel tract from Simon be to someone in his community? Imagine one of the secretaries at the lumberyard receiving a tract from Simon or someone in his congregation. That secretary would not know Simon for his devotion to God's kingdom, but for his desire to hang on to as much of this world's wealth as possible. If you were that secretary, would you be interested?

Or imagine being one of his employees and picking up a tract in the break room. You sit down and start reading an excellent article about the shortness of this life, the importance of living for eternity, and the foolishness of focusing on temporal pleasures. Yet your boss is on vacation in Hawaii, spends several weeks each year at his second home, and is pursuing earthly fulfillment as passionately as anyone you know. Whatever the tract might say, would you believe that your boss has found a treasure in Jesus Christ worth far more than earthly pleasure?

What about the attorney? He sees Simon as one of the slickest businessmen in the community—a man who knows how to make this material world work in his favor. But what if this attorney becomes disillusioned with life? What if he tires of the empty, materialistic charade being played out by his fellow businessmen? If he comes to a point where he is desperate for truth, do you think he will contact Simon? Why would he?

Potential to Demonstrate

Most of us have struggled with our occupations and the amount of time they demand of us. We rush off to our jobs every morning, pouring energy into providing for our families. At times we wonder, *Is something out of balance here?* If our goal is just to put food on the table and keep the bills paid, are our occupations consuming more of our focus than God intended? Many could just work a few days a week and still survive.

But what if God has something much greater in mind? What if He desires our occupations to accomplish more than just supplying our physical needs?

When the Apostle Paul left the church at Ephesus for the last time, he gave a passionate plea to the newly formed church. He told them they would not see him again on this earth, warned them of coming deception, and challenged them to watch for doctrinal heresy. It was a fervent, emotional address that concluded with the group praying and weeping together before accompanying him to the waiting ship. I have often overlooked Paul's final words in this touching discourse. Amazingly, he finished by speaking about his occupation and use of material things.

> I have coveted no man's silver, or gold, or apparel. Yea, ye yourselves know, that these hands have ministered unto my necessities, and to them that were with me. I have shewed you all things, how that so laboring ye ought to support the weak, and to remember the words of the Lord Jesus, how he said, It is more blessed to give than to receive."[a]

---

[a] Acts 20:33–35

In these final words to this fledgling church, there are several points we should note:

1. Paul's lack of interest in accumulating wealth was obvious. He had lived in such a way that no one could accuse him of desiring more silver or gold.

2. Paul had supported himself by working. Even though he was an apostle and much of the world was still waiting for the Gospel, he felt strongly enough about this point that he expended time and energy to be self-supporting.

3. Paul had used his work as a tentmaker to drive home an important truth: every person who is able should work physically to support himself and those who are weak and unable to provide for themselves.

This last point has impressed me. If ever a missionary should not have had to focus on making money and supporting himself, surely it would have been Paul. Most of the known world had never heard the Gospel, so why would he sit around making tents while a lost world was waiting? Were his priorities out of line? Or have we missed the potential that our occupations have, as Paul said, to show something to those who observe?

A Contagious Vision
Several years ago I sat down with a young father who was a manager in a local factory. We discussed his job as well as his views regarding business. In his youth he had been employed by a man who was difficult to get along with and hard on his employees. When he left that job and started working in the factory where he was currently employed, he came with a very negative attitude. He saw business as a necessary evil, and owners as selfish and greedy.

But working in this factory had completely changed his perspective. He shared some of the ways his employer tried to improve the lives of his men and point them toward the kingdom of God. The company frequently offered seminars, paying the men to attend. Here the men learned how to be godly leaders in their churches and homes, as well as at work. The company also provided literature for employees to take home to teach and encourage their families.

This young father had worked in this factory for about five years. He had come seeing no connection between a man's business and his spiritual life, but his view of business was transformed simply by observing his employer's life.

This was a large company, and everyone knew the owner could afford to live however he wanted. He could have taken exotic vacations, bought a second home, or lived in a mansion. Instead, he proved repeatedly that his primary motivation was living for God. The young factory manager shared how observing his boss's dedication impacted his life. He now manages over forty men, and instead of seeing them as a necessary means for production, he sees them as children of God—something he learned from his boss. He spoke about his work with enthusiasm. "This job has given me a tremendous opportunity to minister to a large circle of people every day!" Clearly, his employer's goal of using business for the kingdom was contagious!

There is great risk in becoming too involved in business, yet God desires that we produce and provide for our families. I believe He intends that we use our occupations as platforms to demonstrate kingdom principles.

Is your church using business as a vehicle for evangelism? And what about the risk? Are you holding your businessmen accountable, not only for how they use their wealth, but also for how they conduct business?

Business is a wonderful platform for outreach, but it can also be a great deterrent. If we are going to reach out to our communities through our occupations, we need to be asking some questions. And if your congregation is unable to discuss this issue, the root of the problem might be deeper than you think.

CHAPTER FOURTEEN

Connecting Vocations with Vision

Historically, churches have stayed away from speaking into a successful businessman's life or questioning how he conducts his business or uses his money. I propose we rethink this position. The best place for a brotherhood to be is not far away, but up close to the businessman. This is safest for both the businessman and the brotherhood.

Recently I was invited to teach a class of men of varying ages from several conservative churches. Most were in their twenties and thirties, with a few in their fifties and sixties. Some owned their own businesses, while others were employees. After a few days of teaching, I asked the class several questions.

"How many of you believe it would be good to bless the businessmen in your congregations and also hold them accountable?"

Every hand went up. All those present could imagine ways in which the kingdom could be expanded through business. But the second question caused some furrowed brows.

"How many of you believe your local church would be interested in moving that direction?"

After some thought, only two hands went up, and a spirited discussion ensued. Some said that wealthy businessmen in their congregation would not want accountability, while others were concerned that too much transparency might be unhealthy—that knowing the details about everyone's financial situation might create unnecessary tension. Several commented that even their church leaders would not be comfortable having this kind of discussion. Some of their leaders were wealthy businessmen themselves, and it might be awkward.

Example of the Early Church
Maybe this is where your church is. It would just be too hard, too uncomfortable, and too extreme to do something like that. But before you ditch the concept and decide that financial transparency isn't feasible, be honest enough to confess that your vision is radically different from the early church. Financial transparency was one of their first responses to the Gospel.

As I compare the challenges of surviving in our materialistic culture with the challenges the early church faced, it seems obvious that our need for accountability is much greater today. We are pressured on every side, and if we want to use our occupations effectively for the kingdom, then we need to look more closely at ways we can hold each other accountable. I don't think this will look the same for every congregation, so I would like to consider several options.

Financial Transparency
At the bottom of the chart on the next page is a continuum showing a range of transparency options. Starting on the left side is openness only in times of financial crisis. In other words, don't share any information until your business is in trouble. Many churches operate like this.

Moving to the right, toward greater transparency, is asking all members of a congregation to share their amount of debt. There are different ways this can take place. Some share this information

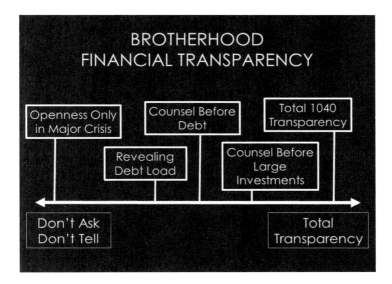

with the brotherhood, while others report only to their deacon. This provides an opportunity for accountability, forewarns those who might be called on for assistance, and permits the deacon to watch for trends. Moving on to the right are more options, all the way to total transparency by submitting yearly tax returns.

Opinions will differ, and my goal is not to push for one method over another. The point is this: if your vision is just to use your businesses to provide for your families and send money to foreign missions, then go out, work hard, and make as much money as you can.

But if your goal as a brotherhood is to use every part of your lives, including how your businesses operate, to demonstrate Jesus to the surrounding culture, then it is essential to think about financial transparency and accountability. Just one business providing poor service or going bankrupt could doom your purpose.

> Are money, possessions, and business outside the scope of brotherhood discussion?

Is your church able to discuss

this topic? Or are money, possessions, and business outside the scope of brotherhood discussion? Again, the point here is not which model of accountability is best. There are good reasons a church should be cautious about sharing too much information, especially with younger individuals who are enthusiastic about not laying up treasures on earth but who may not understand cash flow and how much money it takes to operate a business. But the question is, Can you talk about the options? Is your church serious enough about reaching out locally to have this kind of discussion?

Relationship to the Business World

There are other blessings to openness regarding wealth and occupations. Many men have difficulty knowing their own gifts and abilities. On the chart below is another continuum showing a range of occupational options. On the left is Servant Sam. He is employed by others, goes home at five o'clock, and believes this is where he is called to be. At the other end of the continuum is Production Paul. He loves business and is always looking for opportunities to expand.

Many men struggle to know where they belong on this continuum. I have worked with men who thought they were Production

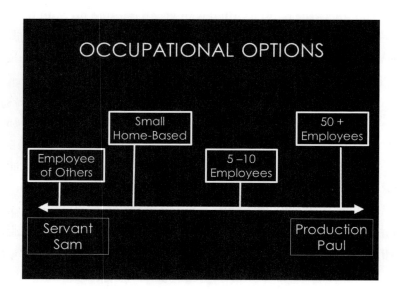

Pauls, but should have been employed by someone else. I have also seen employees who had gifts to administrate a business, but they had no one to encourage and mentor them. Some churches even frown on ownership, and young men sense that avoiding business ownership is somehow more spiritual. This can be a problem, especially in church plants where good jobs for men are scarce.

But what if brothers could come alongside a young man and help him find his place? Imagine the blessing of coming together and discussing how each brother could use his gifts and resources to meet community needs.

Vision Drift

There is another reason accountability is needed in our churches—we tend to drift. Earlier we looked at two reasons we tend to move in our relationship with culture. These also apply in our relationship with the business world. Again, we tend to move toward what we love and away from what we despise.

If a man loves the status of operating a large corporate enterprise and the wealth big business can generate, he will tend to slowly drift toward big business. This does not mean that every large enterprise is a result of these motives, but we need to understand the danger.

On the other hand, a community needs businesses. If a man despises larger businesses, he will retreat and may neglect his gifting. Since we are not always good at analyzing our motives, it is much better if a community discuss these issues and helps men use their God-given gifts while maintaining a balance on this continuum. When a church can both bless the businessman and hold him accountable, businesses can be a great blessing to the kingdom and local community.

Jim is a business owner who has excellent administrative gifts. He started with nothing, and over a period of thirty years has built a large, profitable business. Today Jim spends his time traveling, enjoying outdoor activities, and relaxing in his vacation home. Jim is living the American dream. He worked hard, managed well, and now enjoys the fruit of his labors.

Jim also belongs to a conservative church that holds him accountable in many ways. They are very interested in what he wears, the color of his car, and how he combs his hair. His church knows how to hold members accountable—except in business and wealth. Somehow the fact that Jim has spent millions of dollars in self-centered pursuits is not up for discussion. While other minute details of his life are watched quite closely, this area is off limits. How do you think the early church would have regarded a situation like this?

I want to be very clear. I am not proposing that every church should immediately start sharing every detail and have complete financial transparency. I am suggesting, however, that every church should be able to prayerfully discuss and decide what level of transparency and accountability would help them follow the vision to which God is calling them.

The Gray Areas

Businessmen are called upon to make many decisions, and the church today needs safe places where these men can receive counsel. Building contractors will need to decide if they should build luxurious homes, extravagant kitchens, or homes for individuals involved in immoral lifestyles. Would it be acceptable if they, as followers of Jesus, would help construct liquor stores, adult bookstores, or establishments they wouldn't feel good supporting? Do we have any responsibility for a product's end use?

How about farmers growing grapes that will be used for wine, raising hops for beer, or harvesting corn to make whiskey? Does any of this matter? Should the owner of a construction company build a Mormon church house or work on a military project? "After all," a business owner could argue, "if I don't do it, someone else will."

These are just a few of the many dilemmas that businessmen face, but employees are not exempt either. Choosing to work for someone else can sometimes make these decisions even more complex. Some of these questions are not as simple as they first appear, and my goal is not to provide pat answers. Rather, I want to point out the great need that men have for a support group. And I can think of no better support group than a local brotherhood.

A Few Good Men

It may not always be prudent to have an open discussion involving the entire congregation, but can't we find a few good men? The Apostle Paul, when writing to the church at Corinth about lawsuits, asked this rhetorical question. "Is it so, that there is not a wise man among you?"[a] Is no one capable of providing judgment, sound wisdom, and guidance when facing difficult questions? God has placed wonderful gifts within the body of Christ, but many times they go untapped. Can Spirit-filled men within our churches prayerfully consider these kinds of questions and walk alongside businessmen who need guidance?

Imagine a young man in your congregation who has an obvious gift for business. Everything he touches seems to make money, and he wants to use this gift for the glory of God. What are you going to do? You know there is both danger and blessing in this young man's gift. So how would you respond? Typically, a church will stand back and watch. If he is financially successful, he will be expected to fund needs within the church and provide jobs for young men. If he uses his resources in selfish ways, people will shake their heads and privately comment on the dangers of wealth. Can't we do better than that?

The Call to Leadership

In Paul's first letter to Timothy, he said, "Charge them that are rich in this world, that they be not highminded, nor trust in uncertain riches, but in the living God, who giveth us richly all things to enjoy; that they do good, that they be rich in good works, ready

---

[a] 1 Corinthians 6:5

to distribute, willing to communicate; laying up in store for themselves a good foundation against the time to come, that they may lay hold on eternal life."[b]

We are familiar with this passage, but often we neglect to notice who was being addressed. I hear people say, "Paul told the rich members in the church that they should not be high-minded."

But Paul's message was not to rich people in the church; rather, it was a message to Timothy, a leader in the church at Ephesus. Paul was telling him it was his responsibility to hold wealthy members accountable for what they had been given. Before you lightly dismiss the need for financial accountability in the church, look closely at this command to leadership.

Tapping into the Potential

Maybe the thought of holding businessmen in your church accountable sounds extremely difficult. Maybe even bringing up the topic for discussion seems out of reach. I challenge you to prayerfully consider the untapped potential for the kingdom that resides in our businesses. If you are a leader, are you fulfilling this instruction given by the Apostle Paul? When was the last time you came alongside a wealthy brother in your congregation to provide accountability? This message to Timothy is insightful. Paul begins by warning about the dangers of wealth, and this is still needed in our churches. Wealth brings many pressures, and leadership should provide caution, but it does not end there. Timothy was also commanded to encourage the rich to use their wealth and look for ways to build the kingdom.

Our goal should not be to just rail on the problems of materialism and capitalism. We should also demonstrate a better way with our lives and businesses. This can happen if local churches will prayerfully discern God's will and connect their vocations to that vision.

---

[b] 1 Timothy 6:17–19

PART FOUR

Are We LIMITING God?

CHAPTER FIFTEEN

Limiting God

The faucet at our kitchen sink has caused ongoing frustration. It looks good on the outside, but over time the hot water gradually loses pressure and the output is reduced. Eventually there is a noticeable difference between the two sides. But this change in water flow on the hot side happens over several months, and it is only by moving the handle back and forth between hot and cold that its loss of pressure becomes apparent. Since I usually notice mechanical issues before my wife does, I first go through a time of denial, and then a period of hoping she hasn't noticed. I hate to bring the issue to her attention for a very good reason: I understand the problem, and I don't like the solution.

Resolving the problem involves cleaning out the things that lurk in dark cupboards under kitchen sinks, lying on my back, scooching into a dark, cramped space. It means craning my neck, reaching into the murky unknown, and trying to get two wrenches to work in concert without skinning my knuckles, all the while feeling water run down my arm. Then I have to remove and clean a small in-line filter, put the fittings back together, and extricate myself from the bowels of the cabinet without causing additional damage. If I am successful, the water flow will be restored, there will be no leaks, and my wife will be happy.

It is surprising what a small amount of foreign material it takes to create all this disruption. I think I would feel better if I removed large quantities of debris from the filter. Instead, I usually find just a few particles of rust, the result of galvanized pipes deteriorating farther up the line. We have a good well and a strong pump. Producing consistent pressure to the water line is not a problem. The pipes running through our house are large enough to fill a bathtub in a few minutes. We have no problem with supply. Given all this, it is frustrating when all that power and potential is hampered by a few flakes of rust.

A Few Flakes of Rust

I wonder if God felt similar frustration as He worked with the children of Israel. God wanted His people to display the beauty of His character and the majesty of His power. Repeatedly, He reminded them that He was blessing them so all the nations could see the beauty of holiness. God has always wanted the entire world to worship Him.[a] But in spite of all the wonderful works God did for the Israelites, they refused to give Him total control. The Psalmist, looking back over those years, wrote these insightful words: "How oft did they provoke him in the wilderness, and grieve him in the desert! Yea, they turned back and tempted God, and *limited the Holy One of Israel.* They remembered not his hand, nor the day when he delivered them from the enemy"[b] (emphasis added).

Did you notice? The nation of Israel limited, or restricted, God's power! Try to wrap your mind around that! A God of such majesty and power that He could speak the entire universe with all its complexities into existence allowed a few of His stiff-necked creatures to limit His power!

---

[a] 1 Chronicles 16:24, Psalm 22:27, Isaiah 66:18
[b] Psalm 78:40–42

Make no mistake. God's will was being done throughout the many fiascos in the wilderness. He could have overruled their wills or demonstrated His majesty in some other way, but He didn't. Instead, He chose to work through mortal men, allowing His power to be limited by their lack of faith. Mere men, like a few flakes of rust, were limiting the flow of God's power.

Jesus expressed a similar thought as He looked over Jerusalem and lamented, "O Jerusalem, Jerusalem, thou that killest the prophets, and stonest them which are sent unto thee, how often would I have gathered thy children together, even as a hen gathereth her chickens under her wings, and ye would not!"[c] God had wanted to do great things. His desire was to pour blessings into that nation—power that would not only have blessed them, but flowed into other nations as well. But their unwillingness and lack of obedience had restricted that flow.

Personally Limiting God's Power

I wonder if God has some similar frustrations as he observes my life. I wonder if He occasionally shakes His head and says, "Gary, Gary, how much could be accomplished if you would simply get yourself out of the way!" I look back at times when my selfishness, my desire to be right, my concern about reputation, or just my lack of faith has restricted God's flow of power just like those few flakes of rust reduced the water flow to a trickle. God has so much He wants to accomplish, and He is well able to perform His will. But He has also given me the ability to restrict the flow.

What about your personal spiritual life? You have been given tremendous promises, and great power is available. You have Bibles, access to God through prayer, and everything you need that "pertains to life and godliness."[d] All that power is at your disposal, but how is the flow? Are your neighbors, coworkers, and family being blessed by God through you? Or are there a few flakes of rust limiting God's power? It doesn't take much. Just a little jealousy, a little bitterness over the past, or a

---

[c] Matthew 23:37
[d] 2 Peter 1:3

little unforgiveness in your heart. Little things. Any one of these little flakes can shut down your effectiveness in God's kingdom.

Corporately Limiting God's Power

Local churches, just like individuals, can restrict the flow of God's power as well. God has provided everything necessary to accomplish His purpose, but churches are able to limit God and restrict the flow of the Holy Spirit. Even more concerning, a church can become completely disconnected from God's power.

We can look back at church history, or at professing Christianity around us, and easily conclude that not everything being done in the name of Jesus has His signature on it. A group of people might call themselves Christians, gather in a nice facility each Sunday for worship, and listen to sermons about serving the Lord, all without being connected to God's power. Jesus said many would come to Him in the judgment convinced they had been serving Him, but in spite of all their "spiritual activity," He had not been involved at all.[e] Some other power had been driving their program. We see this around us and shake our heads, but could this occur in *my* church?

The early church had barely begun when a series of sobering messages from the Lord Jesus Himself came to seven churches through the Apostle John. In each letter Jesus said He had been closely observing their activities, and with most of them He wasn't very pleased. The Church had just gotten started, people who had seen the Lord Jesus were still alive, and yet churches were being warned that they had already strayed from God's original purpose. If this can happen to the vibrant early church we read about in Acts, then it can also happen to us.

Of course, we can look back and assume their problems were simply a result of not having access to the Bible. Or we might conclude that they struggled because they didn't have the opportunity to look back over history and learn from the mistakes of the past. There may be some

---

[e] Matthew 7:21–23

truth in these observations, but as the New Testament writers looked forward and prophesied, there is little to indicate that they saw smooth sailing ahead for the church. In fact, their writings convey the exact opposite. All of them gave warnings. It is easy to skip over Scriptural quotations in a book, but I encourage you to take time to read these passages. They give a picture of what the apostles were seeing as they looked ahead to our time.

Notice Paul's warning to Timothy regarding the prevailing culture in the last days:

> This know also, that in the last days perilous times shall come. For men shall be lovers of their own selves, covetous, boasters, proud, blasphemers, disobedient to parents, unthankful, unholy, without natural affection, trucebreakers, false accusers, incontinent, fierce, despisers of those that are good, traitors, heady, highminded, lovers of pleasures more than lovers of God.[f]

Additional caution comes later in the letter regarding heresy in the professing church:

> For the time will come when they will not endure sound doctrine; but after their own lusts shall they heap to themselves teachers, having itching ears; and they shall turn away their ears from the truth, and shall be turned unto fables.[g]

Peter weighs in, prophesying that men will challenge God's Word and promises:

> Knowing this first, that there shall come in the last days scoffers, walking after their own lusts, and saying, Where is the promise of his coming? for since the fathers fell

---

[f] 2 Timothy 3:1–4
[g] 2 Timothy 4:3, 4

asleep, all things continue as they were from the beginning of the creation.[h]

John says one of the hallmarks of the last days will be men who oppose Christ:

> Little children, it is the last time: and as ye have heard that antichrist shall come, even now are there many antichrists; whereby we know that it is the last time.[i]

Jude, with a message very similar to Peter's, reminds believers that the consistent message of the apostles has been that men will increasingly mock God and His message in the last days:

> But, beloved, remember ye the words which were spoken before of the apostles of our Lord Jesus Christ; how that they told you there should be mockers in the last time, who should walk after their own ungodly lusts.[j]

If you took the time to read through these warnings, you should be sobered. The message is clear. The apostles saw major challenges coming in the last days. It would be foolish for us to assume that the path for the church in our time will be easy, that the true church of our day will calmly glide along, coasting into the harbor on smooth water at the end of time. Those early church leaders warned of storms, rough seas, and potential shipwreck.

So what are the challenges of our day? We know God has a purpose for His church and has provided the power to perform His will. Jesus even promised to be with us to the end.[k] But how might our vision be limiting God? What flakes of rust might hinder His will from being accomplished collectively in our churches?

---

[h] 2 Peter 3:3, 4
[i] 1 John 2:18
[j] Jude 1:17, 18
[k] Matthew 28:20

CHAPTER SIXTEEN

Current Challenges

George sighed as he leaned back in his chair, staring at the fire in our woodstove and pondering the question before responding. George lived in the middle of a large concentration of conservative churches. He had stopped in for the night and had been sharing some of his concerns.

"George, if you could push a button and change one thing in your church, what would it be?" I had asked.

It was a simple question, and yet the sober look on George's face showed his difficulty in narrowing it down to just one issue. He had shared many concerns that troubled him. How could he reduce all his concerns to a single point?

George dearly loved his congregation and had no interest in moving or changing fellowships. He believed God had called him and his family to serve where they were. Neither was there any lack of energy or activity in his congregation. Meetings were well-attended and the singing was enthusiastic. When they announced a work day for one of their members, there was no shortage of enthusiastic workers. When word went out regarding some church function, the response was wonderful, and if food was needed, more than enough was brought. If money was lacking in the church treasury or in their private school, people were always willing and ready to help. George felt blessed to live in a setting where so many people cheerfully shared.

But George finally narrowed his thoughts down to one concern: all this energy was being expended to bless their own members, families, and children. Everything was focused on themselves. It was so different from Jesus' example!

Of course, they talked about the importance of reaching out to others. Every good church talks about that. Occasionally some even went to a prison, got involved in some inner-city outreach program, or purchased some literature to pass out. But George's congregation would be shocked if someone from their community found the Lord through their efforts and joined their church. And they would be even more surprised if one such convert could integrate fully into their culture.

After thinking for a while, George responded, "I think what bothers me is the difference between the vision of my congregation and that of the early church. Those first believers were actively involved in the lives of their neighbors. When congregations started up in new cities, they were built with people who came from idolatry. But we are far from that. Just take a look at my church directory. It has the same last names it had fifty years ago!"

George paused before continuing. "But what bothers me the most is the impossibility of discussing this fact. If I could push a button and change just one thing, I would like to see us lose our fear of open dialogue regarding what God might have in mind for our church."

Fear of Open Dialogue
The Gospel of Jesus Christ has the power to transform people's lives. That message goes out Sunday after Sunday across pulpit after pulpit, and there is no question that it is a powerful Gospel. Neither is there

any doubt that spiritual needs abound. We are surrounded by neighbors living meaningless lives and chasing pleasure in myriad ways, attempting in vain to fill the emptiness within. If you live close to a town of any size, you are not far from divorced or single moms left with children and trying to cope with life, men who have made poor financial choices and need to learn basic life skills, and visionless young people roaming the streets with nothing productive to do. We repeatedly say that the Gospel is the answer to all these issues. So why isn't this great power connecting with this great need? And why is there a fear of open dialogue about this shortcoming?

Congregations are different, and there may be several reasons why it is difficult to have open discussion regarding church vision. One reason may simply be current workload. In George's church, people are very busy helping others within the church. There are always widows, struggling church youth, and individuals who need prayer and counseling. By the time the needs of the church are taken care of, there seems to be little energy left for those outside. Over time this becomes normal. The original vision shrinks, the ministry target becomes no larger than the existing church, and the goal of the church becomes little more than nurturing its own families. Is this really what God has in mind?

Imagine visiting a hospital. You walk up and down the corridors visiting patients, and after a while you begin to realize something is strange. It's very busy, yet every patient you interview is an employee of the hospital. You meet nurses taking treatment for cancer, doctors recovering from surgery, and maintenance workers in

line at the hospital pharmacy to fill their prescriptions. All are hospital employees receiving treatment, hoping to get back to work soon.

Leaving the hospital, you ask people on the street about it. One lady says she went to the emergency room once and was impressed. It was well organized and appeared efficient, but after waiting several hours, she left. The staff didn't seem to have time to treat her problem. A man says he had heard that to receive treatment, you needed to be an employee there. A homeless man shakes his head. "I would love to be admitted, but they wouldn't want a dirty fellow like me."

This is not a perfect analogy, but there are some similarities between this hospital and some of our churches. The church, like a hospital, is meant for more than just taking care of its own. There is nothing wrong with hospitals admitting their own employees. In fact, that should be their first responsibility. But when their purpose narrows and they are treating *only* their own staff, something is wrong. So what should a hospital like this do?

> The church, like a hospital, is meant for more than just taking care of its own.

I suggest the first step is for the administration to meet and discuss their goals. Why was this hospital started? What was the impetus behind all the energy and outpouring of resources? There should be staff meetings and open dialogue, because something isn't right! Hospitals were designed for more than just taking care of staff.

The same is true in our churches. If we find our churches, like this hospital, focusing only on internal needs, can we have open dialogue? Can we go back to the early church and honestly compare its purpose to ours?

As I have talked with leaders of various conservative churches about this need for open dialogue, there is obvious hesitation. Their time is already consumed with running from hospital room to hospital room to doctor their own people. They feel understaffed and are not sure their churches could even survive a discussion on vision. Who knows what some of their young radicals might suggest? It is much more comfortable keeping church business meetings controlled by creating an agenda before each meeting, sticking to it, and never letting the discussion get outside of predetermined boundaries.

But I suggest that fear of open dialogue is one of the flakes of rust that clogs the flow of power in our churches.

Knowing versus Doing

We come from different backgrounds and experiences. Some come from church settings where little emphasis was placed on education or knowledge. Church life consisted of keeping the traditions of the previous generation and reacting to the perceived failures of other fellowships, but little thought was given to what the Scriptures actually teach. In some areas Bible study was frowned on, since those who went down that road ended up disrespecting church leaders and authority. Over time apathy and a lack of interest in Biblical truth crept in. It was implied, if not stated outright, that church members should just keep doing what they had been told. Too much learning could be dangerous.

In reaction, men of God rose up and spoke the truth with godly zeal. They pointed out the absurdity of discouraging people from reading and studying the Word of God. They encouraged their children to focus on daily Bible reading, Bible study guides, and Bible study groups. In reaction to the spiritual deadness of the past, they made a tremendous effort to better educate themselves in Scriptural truth.

Today young children go to Sunday school, youth attend Bible schools, and adults attend an astonishing variety of seminars focused on specific topics. Study Bibles, parallel Bibles, exhaustive concordances, and Greek lexicons have been used for years, and with the introduction of electronics, all this can be at your fingertips no matter where you are.

There is still a great need for study, research, and expository preaching. But it is possible to satisfy ourselves with continued learning and forget the importance of simple obedience to what we already know. Learning and studying can become ends in themselves, and being able to express and articulate my beliefs can provide a false inner satisfaction that I am pleasing God. Knowing is a start, but it isn't the same as doing what He says.

I enjoy reading, researching, and listening to inspiring messages, but I have been sobered to realize how easy it is for me to feel fulfilled after hearing a good sermon. Somehow just listening to it seems like "spiritual activity" and gives me the sense of having accomplished something. But where did I get the idea that knowing God's will was synonymous with doing it? Jesus said just the opposite. He reminded His disciples that with learning comes responsibility. Notice His words:

> And that servant, which knew his lord's will, and prepared not himself, neither did according to his will, shall be beaten with many stripes. But he that knew not, and did commit things worthy of stripes, shall be beaten with few stripes. For unto whomsoever much is given, of him shall be much required: and to whom men have committed much, of him they will ask the more.[a]

God intends that we do what we know, yet it is easy to become distracted. One of the areas that can sidetrack a believer, or even an entire congregation, is an undue focus on Biblical prophecy. I believe God intends that we study prophetic passages, try to imagine how things might work out, and prayerfully consider how current events might play into the final showdown of the world. But we can become preoccupied with things that have not been revealed

---

[a] Luke 12:47, 48

while neglecting things that have. There is so much to be done for the kingdom right now in each of our neighborhoods. Should we neglect the hurting around us while attempting to prove that our particular view about the timing of future events is superior to someone else's?

Early Christianity was far different. Around A.D. 200 one of those early believers said, "We do not speak great things; we live them!"[1] Today's Christianity would be laughed at for making that kind of claim, but the Romans didn't laugh when the early Christians said it. They knew it was true. Those first believers were serious about following Jesus in daily life, not just knowing more about Him. We must start living out what we know.

Comparing Our Church with Others

The Apostle Paul's message to the church at Corinth was clear. Comparing ourselves to others is not wise. "For we dare not make ourselves of the number, or compare ourselves with some that commend themselves: but they measuring themselves by themselves, and comparing themselves among themselves, are not wise."[b]

In spite of this clear teaching, I have been amazed at my ability to take comfort in the failure of others. Something inside me says that deficiency in my brother means my spiritual warts are not as ugly as I had first imagined. I can read the words of Jesus and become convicted, but my mind quickly goes to the fact that others aren't taking these words very seriously either. Unless I am careful, that prompting of the Spirit quickly evaporates. This tendency also exists within our churches.

Where there is a high concentration of conservative churches, it is common for them to be defined by slight differences and to be obsessed with constant monitoring. One group makes a slight change, and adjoining fellowships analyze where this trend is heading. Though it is wise to learn from the errors of others, God's

---

[b] 2 Corinthians 10:12

purpose for His church is much loftier than groups sitting around comparing lists and analyzing each other's church standards.

Are we, as individuals and churches, getting our direction from the Bible by the guidance of the Spirit? Or are we primarily reacting to the actions of others? This tendency can be deadly to the vibrant vision God has for His church. We compare the vibrancy in the book of Acts to our personal lives or our local church and become convicted. We need revival! But our minds soon move to the brother or the church down the road. We are doing some things better than they are, so we grow complacent. The call of the Spirit for higher ground is forgotten, and another opportunity is lost.

CHAPTER SEVENTEEN

Current "Christian" Cultural Challenges

We live in an accelerated age. Americans use GPS to find the shortest route home, mobile phones to make the best use of driving time, and garage door openers to avoid the inconvenience and lost time in opening the door manually. Time management is a favorite topic in books and business seminars. Everyone is in a hurry to squeeze more into a day, and consequently, almost every facet of our lives has sped up.

In the 1950s and 1960s the average television commercial was one minute long. People were willing to sit for an entire sixty seconds and listen to a marketer explain why his brand of dish soap was superior. As our world accelerated, advertisers were forced to change, moving to thirty-second spots in the early 1970s. In the 1980s, fifteen-second commercials became popular, and today companies are experimenting with ten- and even five-second spots on television.[1] But for many viewers, even these brief interruptions are too long. They purchase devices that record programs and allow them to watch the show later without commercials.

While you may not be influenced by television or have given much thought to the length of advertisements, rest assured that the cultural forces driving this change are impacting your life in other ways.

Time is money, we are told, and the search is on for techniques or products that decrease the time required to complete tasks. This sense of urgency is contagious. I find myself impatient when the person in front of me doesn't immediately start moving at a green light. A few extra seconds feels intolerable, and my human tendency toward impatience is bolstered by another theme of our day: "You deserve better than this!"

Technology, with all its benefits, has encouraged and fostered impatience. We have come to expect instant results. Why wait by the mailbox when you can send a message electronically? Why take the time to read a book when there's YouTube? Why endure the pain of working on that difficult relationship when you already have more "friends" on Facebook than you can keep up with? Electronic interaction is much easier and quicker. With one stroke of a button you can "unfriend" them and move on.

This instant society promising immediate results has affected our spiritual lives as well. Why sit quietly with the Word of God when multitudes of books, podcasts, and websites offer answers to your spiritual questions? Come across a difficult verse? Just ask Google. This results in a scarcity of believers who are willing to think deeply.

We shake our heads at the scarcity of Bibles in many countries. We hear stories of churches where single pages of Scripture are passed around because few people have a Bible. But sometimes I wonder who is really impoverished. Is it the man who has only one page, but has taken time to memorize, study, and apply it? Or is it the one who has shelves of Bible versions and study guides, yet fails to take time to meditate on a verse and think deeply about what God is calling him to do?

How might this cultural pressure for instant information and gratification be affecting the body of Christ?

Personal Independence

My parents, for some unfathomable reason, insisted on a balanced diet. This included raw vegetables, green salad, and other items that my young mind ruled inedible. I knew I shouldn't argue with God, but sometimes I seriously doubted His pronouncement on the third day of Creation. Was He really including lettuce when He said everything He had created was good?

Occasionally my parents would stop at a restaurant. This was a high point in my formative years, and my favorite was the buffet. Here, assuming I could escape my mother's all-seeing eye, I could make my own selections. I can still picture walking along that well-lit buffet. The options seemed limitless, and I was in charge. I could decide what kind of meat I ate, whether I wanted salad, and how much dessert I would take.

Today, walk into most all-you-can-eat buffets and you will quickly discover that some of us never grow up. We can eat all we want, and our profiles proclaim that we want more than we need. (My mother would have something to say about this!) Ironically, today I enjoy the very types of food I despised in my youth. And I have come to realize that I was not as wise then as I thought I was.

Our Western culture admires personal independence. We have a high regard for the man who knows what he wants, knows how to get it, and doesn't rely on anyone else to achieve his goals. But I wonder if we understand how devastating this is to our spiritual lives and churches. I see many individuals who are serious about their Christian lives, yet seem incapable of surviving long in any one congregation. Like a little boy turned loose at a smorgasbord and searching for the food that fits his taste, they hop from church to church, seemingly unable to come under any ecclesiastical authority. Their list of grievances is long. That leadership was overbearing, while this pastor didn't know how to lead. This church had too much emphasis on youth programs, while that one had such a strong emphasis on home life that their children were awkward social misfits. Finally, after many trips up and down the church buffet without finding that perfect church, many give up. No one, it seems, is doing it correctly. So they withdraw and worship at home.

Surrounding culture, mainstream media, and marketing agencies constantly remind us not to do anything we don't enjoy. Life is short, we are told, so why spend it being miserable? You don't enjoy your occupation? Move on and find another job. Your wife is not fulfilling your needs? Get a divorce; there are plenty of other women out there. Carried over into church life, this message fits nicely with our human desire to rebel against authority. Not satisfied with your church? Tell the leaders, and if they don't see it your way, move on. The buffet table is long, and there are plenty of other churches to choose from. This self-focus, left unchecked, is deadly to vibrant church life. But the idea that life should be easy seeps into theology as well. After all, if life centers around our happiness, shouldn't the path to God be easy as well?

"All You Gotta Do"

As a young man I remember hearing a song sung by a gospel group with a country western twang. I don't remember all the words, but the line that has stuck with me through the years is this: "All you gotta do is trust and pray and believe—you must believe!" Sometimes we refer to this as "easy believe-ism," and sadly, much of what we see and hear coming out of the current "Christian" culture reminds me of this song. The Gospel of Jesus Christ has been reduced to a sketchy belief in the Bible and a mental acceptance of His work on the cross, with the goal of escaping hell. This weak doctrinal soup has permeated our "Christian" world, and since a mental assent and a verbalized belief is "all you gotta do" to escape hell, roughly 75 percent of Americans profess to be Christian[2] and believe they are heaven bound.[3]

This theology has influenced almost every church in America in some way. Consider our vocabulary and how we speak of conversion.

In the early church conversion was linked to a change of life—it literally meant something had changed. Notice how the writer of Acts describes this transformation. "Then they that gladly received his word were baptized.... And they continued steadfastly in the apostles' doctrine."[a] This was not just a one-time event, after which life carried on as usual. Conversion meant something actually changed!

Today we hear conversion described very loosely. Phrases such as, "accepted the Lord," "got saved," "came to the Lord," "joined the church," or "came forward" are used to describe conversion. And while there may not be anything inherently wrong with these phrases, there is a vast difference between deciding to accept and committing to follow.

> There is a vast difference between deciding to accept and committing to follow.

A few years ago I attended a mainline evangelical revival service, complete with an altar call. The minister explained our sinfulness, Christ's righteousness, and the importance of making a decision that night for Christ. He finished by saying something like this: "If you come forward tonight and accept Jesus, you are saved. What you do after that won't affect your standing with God. Salvation is like getting on an airplane for Philadelphia. Once that door is shut and the plane takes off, you are heading to Philadelphia, whether you change your mind or not. And if you decide to accept Christ tonight, you are heading toward heaven, even if you change your mind later on!"

Obviously this minister was a proponent of unconditional eternal security, but look past that for a moment and notice what a person's eternal destiny depended on: a single decision. Making a decision for Christ was "all you gotta do."

---

[a] Acts 2:41, 42

But where in the teachings of Jesus do you find salvation reduced to a one-time decision? Jesus didn't try to downplay the cost of following Him. "Whosoever he be of you that forsaketh not all that he hath, he cannot be my disciple."[b] Those are strong words. When we reduce the Gospel to an isolated decision, rather than total surrender to the lordship of Jesus Christ, we are presenting something other than Christianity, and this is a current "Christian" cultural challenge.

Avoiding Hell

Ask almost any professing believer in America what it means to be saved, and you will probably hear something like this: "It means being saved from hell and going to heaven instead." Now the Scriptures are clear that a literal hell and a literal heaven exist, and every Bible reader of sound mind would prefer heaven. But is being saved synonymous with avoiding hell? Or did God have more in mind than just saving man from eternal damnation?

It is interesting to note that Jesus didn't come to earth preaching, "Repent so you don't have to go to hell," or, "Believe in me and someday you can go to heaven." He came preaching, "Repent: for the kingdom of heaven is at hand."[c] Jesus didn't come just to save us from future pain. He came to establish a kingdom, to overcome Satan's power, and to save us from our own self-centeredness and the bondage of sin.

Jesus' mission was to forgive, restore, and empower, enabling us to exhibit the attributes of God both individually in daily life and collectively through local churches. This is much greater than just saving a man from a future hell. After all, is the man who is held captive by self-centeredness, bound by a love of earthly wealth, or imprisoned by lustful thoughts really saved? God wants us to be free! Not just free from the penalty of future torment, but completely

---

[b] Luke 14:33
[c] Matthew 4:17

free from Satan's grasp. Let's not allow surrounding Christian culture to dictate our theology and reduce God's intent.

N.T. Wright, in his book *Simply Jesus*, addresses our tendency to press verses into our self-centered theology. He speaks of how we misinterpret the message contained in the Beatitudes.

> "Blessed are the poor in spirit: for theirs is the kingdom of heaven" (Matthew 5:3) doesn't mean, "You will go to heaven when you die." It means you will be one of those through whom God's kingdom, heaven's rule, begins to appear on earth as in heaven. The Beatitudes are the agenda for kingdom people. They are not simply how to behave so God will do something nice to you. They are about the way in which Jesus wants to rule the world.[4]

"Jesus Loves Me" is a wonderful song proclaiming a marvelous truth, but if our theology never progresses beyond the reality that Jesus loves us personally, we are missing the beauty and magnificence of the kingdom. "Jesus came to save me" is only a small part of this magnificent story, and overemphasis on this small part can develop into a very self-focused theology.

Perhaps God has saved you and given you the ability to play the trumpet. That is wonderful, and you should play that trumpet with all the strength God has given you. But don't forget, you are called to be part of a larger orchestra, a local church that is producing harmonious and compelling music to a lost and dying world. It is so easy to become enamored with our part in the program and forget that we are a small part of God's larger vision. Our secular society is shouting that it's all about you. Unfortunately this has impacted the "Christian" culture that surrounds us, and this in turn tends to influence our theology.

CHAPTER EIGHTEEN

"So Send I You"

Just outside our back door is an open patio, and on summer evenings it is a great place to sit with the family or enjoy an evening meal. But in the winter we spend little time out there, except for one activity. I enjoy feeding birds. The temperature drops, the snow begins to fall, and my heart goes out to those birds trying to endure the winter. Where are they going to find food, and how will they survive? I scatter seeds on top of a table and wait for the birds to notice. It's amazing how quickly word gets around in the bird world. Before long the birdseed is gone, and I need to replenish the supply.

But something troubles me. I am doing my best to provide for those birds, sacrificing time and money, braving the cold so they can eat. Yet they treat me like their greatest enemy. No matter how slowly I open the back door, they are all gone at the first sound. They fly off to a tree in the yard and watch till I pour out more seed. Then, when I am back in the house, they cautiously return, approaching slowly with furtive glances lest I might still be lurking in the shadows. Can't they see the great effort I'm making for their good? Surely by now we could have developed some kind of understanding or friendly relationship. But no, they love my food, but they don't want me.

God and Gifts

Throughout the Scriptures we see God in a similar quandary. He causes the sun to rise, rain to fall, and seasons to change, making the earth produce a huge variety of food for man's enjoyment. At one point He even put food right outside His people's tents, all the while hoping for a close relationship with them. But just like the birds on my porch, they took the food, yet distanced themselves from the Giver. Prophets like Isaiah pled with Israel, and David tried to explain God's motives, yet very few seemed interested in understanding God or developing a relationship with Him. They liked the gifts more than the Giver. Humanity saw God like those birds on my patio see me—a huge, hulking being that can't quite be trusted, too different to be understood, too frightening to get close to. Yet God wanted men to trust Him, love Him, and commune with Him.

In pursuit of relationship, God sent His Son to earth as a fellow human. He was born in a lowly stable and raised without the trappings of wealth, living in a time of few conveniences in a backwater region of the Roman Empire. Palestine was a place of constant political upheaval, and the Roman Emperor probably wished it would just go away. It wasn't exactly the type of environment you would expect a king to be born into.

Consider the incredible contradictions surrounding His birth. A special star appears, wealthy wise men travel a great distance to pay homage, and the city and king are troubled.[a] In some ways there has never been a more royal birth. Who else in all of history had his own personal star hanging over the delivery room?

Yet He was also born into poverty that even the poorest homeless man could identify with. No room in the inn, a sleepy town evidently oblivious to His arrival, dirty animals, and lowly shepherds as His first visitors. What an amazing entrance into the world! Who but God could have put this astounding and diverse set of circumstances together?

He was born like other men, worked in a shop like other men, ate, slept, and was tempted like other men.[b] Since the Gospels provide so little information on His early years, we forget that He apparently spent most of His life doing carpentry work. In fact, He seemed to have lived so normally that those who knew Him best had the most difficulty believing He was actually God. But remember why He did all this. His Father had sent Him to show by His daily life what God is really like!

The Apostle Paul said that Jesus was the image of the invisible God.[c] That is not just an astonishing statement; it is a cryptic mystery! How can a poor man exemplify a God who owns everything? How can a God capable of speaking the universe into existence be represented by a tiny baby dependent on its teenage mother? Yet even though we struggle to wrap our minds around the paradox, the Bible is clear. Jesus came as the "express image"[d] of His Father. He came to show us what God is really like and to provide a living expression of Himself to His creation.

"So Send I You!"

At the end of His earthly life, just before ascending to the Father,

---

[a] Matthew 2:3
[b] Hebrews 4:15
[c] Colossians 1:15
[d] Hebrews 1:3

Jesus said something that should cause each of us to stop midstride and consider. He transferred this assignment to His followers: "As my Father hath sent me, even so send I you."[e]

How easy it is to read over those few words and carelessly neglect their import! Jesus expected His followers to walk in His footsteps and, through His power, show the Father to the world. So how is the church to do this? How are followers of Jesus, individually and collectively, supposed to provide a living demonstration of what God is really like? Let's start by looking briefly at how Jesus lived His life and how He exhibited the image of the Father.

"Deed and Word"

Two men walking down the road from Jerusalem were trying to explain to a stranger what Jesus had been like. As they reflected on the last several years, they tried to encapsulate His ministry in just a few words. There was so much that could be said, but their summary was that Jesus had been "a prophet mighty in deed and word before God and all the people."[f] Mighty in both *deed and word*.

Notice that they didn't think of Jesus as a man who sat around like the philosophers, imparting lofty themes, dazzling them with brilliant intellect, or using grand vocabulary. When Jesus taught, He used simple stories that any common man could identify with. His words were mighty but simple, and I wonder if this simplicity didn't baffle the disciples. How could He be God and yet use such elementary stories to convey His message?

And what about His deeds?

Philip even came out boldly and asked Him to show them the Father. Jesus responded, "He that hath seen me hath seen the Father."[g] In other words, "Watch my daily life and you will understand God." Jesus had been very involved in their lives, fishing with them, walking along the shore, and sharing meals. Yet He did so

---

[e] John 20:21
[f] Luke 24:19
[g] John 14:9

much more. Think about His life and what it revealed about God.

He touched exiled lepers, ate with society's outcasts, and reached out to Samaritans, showing no class, cultural, or religious discrimination. Jesus even healed a Roman centurion's child, demonstrating total lack of political bias. On the one hand, He loved to be with the poor and seemed to esteem them more than the rich, yet He did not spurn the wealthy. We find Him sharing meals in their homes and even being the honored guest at their banquets. When the rich young ruler came to Him, the account says that Jesus loved him. Jesus didn't discriminate against him simply because he belonged to the upper class.

It seems Jesus crossed just about every boundary and class distinction, whether political, religious, social, or economic. Jesus didn't let these distinctions, so important to men, interfere with His relationships with people. Ignoring the judgment of others, Jesus responded with truth and grace to each person He encountered. His actions clearly demonstrated His Father's opinion of all people. Peter, in the house of Cornelius, while describing Jesus' life and daily activities, said He "went about doing good."[h] And it was against this backdrop of doing good to all men that He taught simple truths that shook the world.

Followers or Fans?

Jesus' actions provided credibility to His words. Even current detractors who refuse to acknowledge Jesus' deity admit that He had a reputation for "doing good" and was an effective teacher. But what about the church He left behind? What is it known for? Is it able to go out and preach with the same credibility? Jesus' words had weight because they were backed by His actions. His love for humanity's natural needs gave credence to His message and provided a clear picture of what God is like. Would you say Christianity today is the same? Are we doing a good job of imitating Jesus and obeying

---

[h] Acts 10:38

His mandate to exhibit the character of God? How does the secular public see the professing Christian community?

> Are we doing a good job of imitating Jesus and obeying His mandate to exhibit the character of God?

One does not have to go very far to answer that question. Many today see modern evangelical Christianity as a giant political action committee that supports military growth, big business, and the Republican Party. Recently I found an anonymous writer commenting on the hypocrisy of American Christianity.

> He (Jesus) spent his life helping the poor, sick, and needy. He embraced those from the lowest rungs of society. . . . He taught love, hope, compassion, and forgiveness. . . . You know, the exact opposite of what Republicans stand for.

It concluded by saying,

> So please stop calling Republicans "Christians." They're not. They worship Reagan, guns, and greed—not Jesus Christ.

This is quite an indictment against nominal Christianity, and this writer is not alone. An increasing number of journalists are standing up and accusing the church of extreme hypocrisy. The huge discrepancy between the teachings of Jesus and the lives of those professing to be His followers is too obvious to be overlooked. Bill Maher is an agnostic writer and television host who loves to publicly point out the flaws in the "Christianity" he sees around him. In one of his talks, labeled *New Rule: Thy Will Be Gun*, which addresses the hypocrisy of calling yourself a follower of Jesus while ignoring His teachings, Bill calls on Americans to quit calling themselves Christians.

He explains by saying,

> If you rejoice in revenge, torture, and war, you cannot say you are a follower of the guy who said love your enemies, and do good to those who hate you. . . . Nonviolence was kind of Jesus' trademark. Kind of his big thing. To not follow that part of it is like joining Greenpeace and hating whales. There's interpreting, and then there's just ignoring. It's just ignoring if you're for torture, as are more evangelical Christians than any other religion."[1]

That's a powerful accusation. Bill Maher concludes by summarizing his assessment of American professing Christians: "You're not Christ's followers, you're just fans!"

Your Local Congregation

We have been sent into our world to reveal the character of God, not just to talk about escaping hell. We have been called to corporately exhibit the very person of Jesus Christ. This is why members of the early church were known as Christ-followers. They were famous for modeling Him in their daily lives. If someone visited your community and asked your low-income neighbors about your church, what would they hear? Are you famous for reaching out and showing love to society's castaways like Jesus was?

If someone visited on a Sunday morning and looked up and down the pews of your church, what would they see? Would they find the poor and the "lepers," society's untouchables? Does your congregation have enough connection with those people that they would feel welcome attending services? Imagine for a moment that Jesus was the pastor or even a member of your congregation. What type of people do you think He would bring with Him each Sunday?

Every congregation should be known for taking care of needs within the church. Just as Jesus focused first on His own Jewish people, we also should ensure that every member is supported and loved. But just like Jesus, we should not stop there. We should also have a deep desire that all men be saved. This will involve more than just walking through town handing out Christian literature. It must include building relationships with our neighbors and demonstrating what God is really like. When this occurs by the power of God's Spirit, beautiful, persuasive music will pour out of our churches and into the communities we live in.

CHAPTER NINETEEN

Programmed Evangelism

Springview Community Fellowship knew they had a problem. Things were not as they had been twenty years earlier when the church was founded. With just a few families back then, everyone had been needed and involved. The church had started with a deep desire to reach out to others in the community, and they had initially experienced growth. Wednesday night services were exciting. Visitors came, long discussions took place in the aisles afterward, and the janitor wasn't sure how to get everyone to leave so he could go home. Members chatted about people they had been working with and discussed ways they could bless others in the neighborhood. Springview was an exciting place to be, and first-time visitors always received warm acceptance and an invitation for lunch.

But over time things had changed. The church grew, people's lives became busier, and that friendly reception the church had once been known for slowly evaporated. Leaders were busy with internal issues, and everyone assumed someone else was taking care of the seekers; consequently, there were fewer first-time visitors seeking truth.

Knowing that change was needed, the pastor called a special

meeting. He outlined the problem, reviewed their history of reaching out in the community, and listened to the members' ideas. Some who had joined from the community spoke of what it had felt like to walk in the door that first time. They talked about the warmth they had sensed in the church and the shock they had felt when they were invited to members' homes for meals. They could tell that this church possessed the love and sense of community they lacked! These factors compelled them to return, and through this little group they had received a different picture of God's character.

A lively discussion followed, suggestions were made, and finally a plan of action was agreed upon. They knew their lives were too busy, and they were not doing as well at showing hospitality as they once had. So they selected a hospitality committee and gave them the task of making visitors welcome. There would be greeters at the door to shake the hand of each visitor, make sure the visitors had a good seat, and even provide them with a welcome packet detailing all the events and programs Springview Community Fellowship offered. Everyone went home that night feeling much better. They had known something was wrong, and now they had a program that addressed the problem.

> Does a hospitality committee replace a hospitable church?

But did it really? Does a hospitality committee replace a hospitable church? It is nice to be welcomed at the door, have a good seat, and even have a good grasp of what the church is about. But will that really replace sitting down in someone's home and sharing together? How much responsibility will the rest of Springview's members feel to make visitors welcome next Sunday?

Early Evangelism

Multiple passages in Scripture show clearly that God intended for the early church to have leaders. These were men ordained by God to oversee the church, take care of physical needs, and fill administrative roles. It is also clear that some men were specifically ordained as evangelists to go out and preach the Gospel. In Acts we read that the church at Antioch sent Saul and Barnabas out. Notice: "As they ministered to the Lord, and fasted, the Holy Ghost said, Separate me Barnabas and Saul for the work whereunto I have called them. And when they had fasted and prayed, and laid their hands on them, they sent them away. So they, being sent forth by the Holy Ghost, departed unto Seleucia; and from thence they sailed to Cyprus."[a]

Though God chooses specific men to do certain tasks, it is also apparent that evangelism was never intended to be relegated to just a few. The desire to reach out will be in the heart of every true believer. Notice how the writer describes the oppression of the church at Jerusalem and the resulting evangelistic effort. "And at that time there was a great persecution against the church which was at Jerusalem; and they were all scattered abroad throughout the regions of Judaea and Samaria, except the apostles."[b]

Persecution is raging; everyone runs to other areas, except for the leaders of the church. They hunker down in Jerusalem. But what is the rest of the church doing while the apostles are still in Jerusalem? The account continues: "They that were scattered abroad went every where preaching the word."[c]

Reaching out to the lost is a natural result of realizing our own condition without Christ and having a fervent desire that others experience the same blessing. It is an integral part of every serious believer. Jesus came "to save that which was lost,"[d] and each of us has been sent out to do the same. But what happens to churches when individual members lose that desire?

---

[a] Acts 13:2–4
[b] Acts 8:1
[c] Acts 8:4
[d] Matthew 18:11

Evangelism = Program

When you think of evangelism, do you think of neighbors, coworkers, and daily interaction with people in your local community? Or does your mind automatically go to projects or programs? There is nothing intrinsically wrong with programs. After all, choosing to have a hospitality committee may turn out to be a blessing for Springview Community Fellowship. But we must understand the inherent risks and dangers of programs. When we cannot conceive of outreach apart from an organized program, the vision of the early church has been lost.

> When we cannot conceive of outreach apart from an organized program, the vision of the early church has been lost.

Recently I sat in a conference where outreach was being discussed. Participants shared many good insights, but as I looked out over the crowd, I couldn't help but wonder what would happen if all these people simply reached out to the people they knew within their own communities. What if each one developed a relationship with one person and brought that person to church in the coming year?

Maybe they already were very involved locally, but sometimes it seems we neglect the obvious. Many excellent programs do tremendous good. They produce Christian literature, teach and train indigenous leaders in foreign countries, and reach out during times of crisis through humanitarian aid. All of these programs are good and should be encouraged, but if we immediately equate outreach with programs, we may be missing God's primary means of evangelism.

So why do our minds go to programs and foreign soil when considering evangelism? I think of several possibilities.

Fish Where Fish Are Biting

It has been said that good fishermen go where the fish are biting, and we may think of foreign countries simply because there is more interest in the Gospel there. While writing this chapter, I received a phone call from a brother who is working in a restricted country. He has seen Muslims coming to Christ, and his voice was filled with enthusiasm. "I feel so blessed to be here! I feel like the Lord has given me a front-row seat as new churches are springing up!"

I hung up the phone and reflected on the difference. It doesn't always seem so exciting here. I have seen local people come to faith as well, but often they come with marriage problems, financial struggles, and relationship issues. Walking with them means late nights, difficult relationships, and sometimes they walk away in the end. Of course, all this can happen in other countries as well, but middle-income, self-centered Americans are not always very interested in a self-denying Gospel.

But do we use this as an excuse? A friend of mine used to say, "You can lead a horse to water, but you can't make him drink. However, you can give him salt to increase his thirst." I suspect part of the reason we see so little thirst for the Gospel locally is because we provide so little salt.

Allow yourself to dream for a moment of an imaginary church that is famous for loving and speaking well of other believers, even though they belong to a different fellowship. Imagine a church where the men have no interest in accumulating wealth, women are unmoved by fashion or fads, and first-time visitors receive a warm and genuine welcome. Don't stop dreaming! The young men are known to be extremely good employees, and its business owners are famous for exceeding their customers' expectations. Stories are passed around through the community of widows being helped, single mothers receiving support, and mourners being comforted.

What you are imagining is a very salty church. And while no man comes to the Father except the Father draws him,[e] maybe

---
[e] John 6:44

our attempts to reach out to others locally would go better if our churches were a little saltier.

Improper Vision

Recently I listened to a young father in a conservative fellowship describe his church's lack of interest in local evangelism. He struggles with it, yet desperately wants to be under authority. He has seen negative results in groups that don't take separation from the world seriously, so he appreciates his leaders' desire to not be swayed by culture. Yet he is trying to come to peace with their view of outreach. It bothers him that he is reluctant to invite people from the community to his church. He senses that many in his congregation would not be very excited about seeing someone come to church who has skin of a different color, struggles with addictions, or is covered with tattoos. He wants to be faithful to New Testament vision, but also supportive of his church leaders. He concluded by saying, "Really, it is fine to reach out in my church, and my leaders won't say anything about it—just as long as you don't tell anyone else what you are doing."

In the days that followed, my mind kept going back to his concluding comment. I suspect his leaders would justify this position by referring to Jesus' teaching about not praying, fasting, or giving alms to be seen of men.[f] But let's be honest. Jesus was not saying we should refuse to pray, fast, or give alms. He was teaching on motives, telling us not to seek praise for doing these things. This applies to every area of life.

What would you think if someone said, "It is okay to read the Bible in your home as long as you don't tell others what you are doing"? Or, "It is fine to teach your children spiritual truths, as long as you don't let it be known"?

We understand that reading the Bible and teaching our children are extremely important. They are central parts of the vision for

---

[f] Matthew 6:1–18

our lives and homes, and we aren't embarrassed to say so. What this young man was actually telling me is this: reaching out locally is really not a central part of our church vision. Can you imagine the church in Acts saying, "It's okay to reach out to your neighbors, but don't let the apostles know about it"? When we arrive at this position, a major part of that early church vision has been lost.

Evangelism as an Appendage

Outreach in the book of Acts was not a program; it was part of their very fiber. Go back through church history and notice what happens when revival breaks out in a church. Whenever you find spiritual revival, it is immediately followed by outreach. When men, convicted by the Spirit of God, repent of their lukewarm lives and pursue the heart of God, the result is predictable. They begin to share with others what they have found, new churches are planted, and the Gospel spreads. But when evangelism becomes an appendage, a tacked-on program that helps us feel better about ourselves, something crucial has been lost.

Reaching out must be part of our core doctrine and an integral part of our purpose. It can be done many ways, using our differing abilities, financial resources, and spiritual gifts. It's sobering to realize that sometimes the poorest people on the globe are better at reaching out to neighbors than those of us who get so distracted in our more affluent settings. Resolve to bless those you come in contact with each day. Show them by your life choices that you have been with Jesus.

There is a difference between building relationships and evangelism. You can do the first without accomplishing the second. But I suggest that starting with hospitality and developing relationships with those whom God places in your life is an excellent way to reach out and reveal the character of God.

Sometimes I hear people say they are "going out to witness tonight." That phrase intrigues me. It makes me wonder what they have been doing during the day. My interest is not to discourage witnessing. Rather, let's expand witnessing to include every part of our lives. When we reduce evangelism to a program or an accessory, we are limiting the vision God has for our churches.

PART FIVE

The POWER and PURPOSE of Oneness

CHAPTER TWENTY

Last Words: Famous or Forgotten?

Few men in history have shaped the scientific world more than Michael Faraday. Born into the home of a poor London blacksmith on September 22, 1791, Michael became one of the most famous scientists the world has ever known. His achievements were even more remarkable in light of the fact that science during this time was a discipline reserved for a privileged class to which Michael did not belong. Though Michael received little formal education, he was blessed with an insatiable desire to learn. Working for a local bookbinder, he bound books by day and read them by night. From this intense desire to learn came an astounding array of discoveries.

Michael is famous for his discoveries in electromagnetism, for being the first to turn chlorine into a liquid, and for discovering benzene. Common items we use today such as electric motors and electric transformers trace their origins back to him. Despite having far less education than his scientific peers, Michael continued to push into new frontiers, even developing new metal alloys. In modern universities, Faraday is still lauded as an exceptional scientist, a man of brilliant intellect. But some important facts are typically left out of his story.

Michael Faraday was a devout Christian, clearly displaying to his community that his first passion was following Jesus Christ. In his older years, as awards and acclaim began to pour in, Michael seemed unmoved. The British Empire offered him knighthood in recognition of his services to science, but he turned it down, saying it was against the Word of God to accumulate riches and pursue worldly reward. He told them he preferred to remain just "plain Mr. Faraday" until the end. Twice he refused to become president of Britain's Royal Society, and when the government offered him a burial site in Westminster Abbey alongside England's kings and queens, Michael rejected the offer. He preferred to be buried in the Highgate Cemetery where the common people were buried.

Last Words

If anyone should have been able to look back at the end of life and rejoice in accomplishments, surely it would be Michael. But it is insightful to notice his last words. Just before he died, someone asked Michael what he thought his occupation might be in the next world. Surely God must have something in mind for this great man. His simple response revealed his heart, his passion, and the driving force behind his life. "I shall be with Christ, and that is enough."[1] His interest in earthly accomplishments wasn't as great as his desire to be with his Lord.

> I shall be with Christ, and that is enough.
> –Michael Faraday

Last words reveal much about a person, and many have gathered around the beds of the dying, hoping to hear their final words. In the Old Testament we read of men like Jacob. His family gathered around and listened to his final prophetic words.[a] Joseph, just before he died, gave final instructions

---

[a] Genesis 49:33

to his family.[b] All through the ages men have listened carefully to last words. Michael Faraday's should be famous. Instead, they have been overlooked by most of the world.

Famous or Forgotten?

Just before leaving this earth and going back to His Father, Jesus spoke some last words as well. To those of us who grew up hearing the Scriptures, they are very familiar. Yet looking around at the church today, it is evident that the powerful import of these words has been lost. We find these words in John 17, and this High Priestly Prayer can be divided into three parts. Notice what was on His heart just before His death.

Jesus begins in the first five verses by reviewing his mission here on earth and asking for strength for His final hour. Then in verses 6–19 He prays for His disciples—this little band of rough men who had followed Him around, arguing who would be the greatest and showing little potential to lead a kingdom. Finally, almost as an emotional appeal to His Father to do the impossible, Jesus prays for His kingdom here on earth. As you consider His final words before going to the cross, try to grasp the glorious vision Jesus had for His church. Notice both His plea for oneness and the impact this unity will have on a lost world.

> Neither pray I for these alone, but for them also which shall believe on me through their word; that they all may be one; as thou, Father, art in me, and I in thee, that they also may be one in us: that the world may believe that thou hast sent me. And the glory which thou gavest me I have given them; that they may be one, even as we are one: I in them, and thou in me, that they may be made perfect in one; and that the world may know that thou hast sent me, and hast loved them, as thou hast loved me.[c]

---

[b] Genesis 50:22–26
[c] John 17:20–23

These last words of Jesus are a powerful mission and vision statement for the church, yet they seem largely forgotten. Jesus was visualizing local groups of believers, intentionally committing themselves in loving relationship, becoming a powerful statement to the world. Their unity was to have a tremendous impact on the world.

In the upper room, just before this prayer, Jesus had made a similar statement. It is a dynamic evangelistic proclamation, yet one of the most neglected verses in the New Testament regarding evangelism and church vision: "By this shall all men know that ye are my disciples, if ye have love one to another." How often have you heard this used as the theme verse at a mission conference?

"By This Shall All Men Know"

Today, unity of believers as God's method to evangelize has fallen out of favor. Being passionate about outreach means going out on your own and holding signs, passing out literature, or supporting a program. Far too often, being spiritually minded means seeing the flaws in a fellowship and moving on to the next. Further, if you want to bring silence to a good discussion in a group of people fired up about reaching out, just try discussing the importance of unity in the church. Why is this? Jesus plainly believed in spreading the Gospel through oneness and love for each other. He spoke of this more than any other method. As one author has correctly stated, "The church is God's evangelism program."[2] So why has pursuing unity in the church become unpopular? Why do we fail to connect oneness in the brotherhood with evangelism on the street?

> Why do we fail to connect oneness in the brotherhood with evangelism on the street?

It is important for our churches to carefully examine these questions if we want to return to the vision Jesus outlined. Most of us can clearly see one error. We talk about that error, analyze the negative aspects of it, and may come to believe our fellowship has embraced this error. In reaction we chart a new course, taking great care to steer clear of the ditch we were in, only to become mired in another. This is why it is important to carefully analyze the issue of unity.

Unity: Appreciating Bones and Muscles
Unity within the body of Christ has been misconstrued to mean everyone should be identical. It is amazing that groups which stress the church being the body of Christ use this analogy to emphasize the power given to the church, yet typically ignore the call for diversity. After all, one of the purposes of the analogy is to stress the importance of individual members having different functions. "If the whole body were an eye, where were the hearing? If the whole were hearing, where were the smelling?"[d] This is not just saying that some are called to be leaders in the church and others are not. It is saying that God has placed tremendous diversity within the body—a wide range of spiritual gifts, an incredible variety of abilities, and a vast assortment of resources. All of these can be useful in the body as we work together in love and remain connected to the Head, Jesus Christ.

Paul's cry in his first letter to the Corinthian church was twofold. First, we need to understand that this diversity in the body is part of God's plan. It is His idea. "But now hath God set the members every one of them in the body, as it hath pleased him."[e] Second, we are to use and develop our gifts, while also appreciating the gifts God has given others. This truth is seen all through the twelfth chapter of 1 Corinthians. For some reason we don't find it difficult to believe that God has given us valuable gifts and important functions in the body. But God is also calling us to place value on the gifts He has given others. One of the reasons we have lost the vision for unity in

---

[d] 1 Corinthians 12:17
[e] 1 Corinthians 12:18

the body is because we have misused this teaching. Paul's teaching was never intended to clone people and make everyone identical.

Beyond Preservation

All of us would agree that those first believers went out with a powerful message, communicated not only by their words but also by their lives. That became a moving testimony. Notice how their unity as a brotherhood was connected with this power.

> And the multitude of them that believed were of one heart and of one soul: neither said any of them that ought of the things which he possessed was his own; but they had all things common. And with great power gave the apostles witness of the resurrection of the Lord Jesus: and great grace was upon them all.[f]

This was just what Jesus had promised: "That they may be made perfect in one; and that the world may know that thou hast sent me."[g]

Too often brotherhood unity has been promoted simply as a way of preserving what we have, as if that is its sole purpose. Many churches interested in preserving their heritage have little interest in integrating seekers from the community into their fellowship.

We have been given a wonderful heritage, and we should preserve the good we have been given. But to an individual who is seriously reading the New Testament and comparing the early church to his local congregation, this preoccupation with preservation can appear self-centered. Is maintaining our heritage the only reason we have brotherhood agreements? What about the masses outside? Why is there so much zeal to maintain little details for the well-being of future generations, yet so little zeal to reach out to neighbors? This can be confusing to a new convert, and to our young people as well.

---

[f] Acts 4:32, 33
[g] John 17:23

We encourage youth to study the Scriptures and read about the early church, but we sometimes get uncomfortable with the penetrating questions this search produces. Is the Lord possibly trying to use some of these questions to convey a message?

Youth often fail to understand how difficult it is to preserve doctrinal truth over time. Sometimes it is hard for them to see the wisdom in certain practices that may seem worthless and archaic. They have yet to learn that only after traditions have been discarded is their value realized. For unity in a brotherhood to work, fervent young people need to understand the importance of patience and being under authority. This will be much easier for them if they see leaders promoting unity for the same reason Jesus did: "That they all may be one; as thou, Father, art in me, and I in thee, that they also may be one in us: *that the world may believe* that thou hast sent me"[h] (emphasis added).

The Carnal and Independent Spirit

Earlier we looked at the fact that Western civilization promotes personal freedom and an independent spirit. Society tells us we should be able to do what we want, when and wherever we want to. This has become the mantra of our society, and woe to the teacher, government official, or even parent who disagrees. Of course this flies in the face of "submitting yourselves one to another."[i] Yet since we are influenced by our surroundings, we shouldn't be surprised if our young people wrestle with this. This desire for personal autonomy is strong and encourages them to resist submitting to a brotherhood. Sometimes overzealous leaders unintentionally provide a platform for young men to justify their lack of submission. This can happen in two ways.

First, imagine a young man who professes to follow the Lord yet secretly desires to be more like the surrounding culture in the area

---

[h] John 17:21
[i] Ephesians 5:21

of dress. He belongs to a group whose dress standard opposes his desires, so he subconsciously longs for an inconsistent leader he can react against to justify his own pursuit of carnality. The strict authoritarian who fails to show concern for the lost provides just what he wants.

On the other hand, imagine a young man with hidden sin who belongs to a conservative church. An emphasis on externals can give him the cover he needs. He feels good about his spiritual life because he is outwardly conforming to a few baseline rules that he has been taught are very important. Everything looks good on the outside, but conformity to standards is covering spiritual apathy within. When leaders place undue emphasis on church authority, or promote oneness for wrong reasons, they make it easy for young men like this to indulge their own hidden carnality.

It is easy to blame rebellious youth who walk away. But is it possible that we who remain are partly at fault? Church unity and brotherhood agreements can be emphasized for wrong reasons. For example, a leader may want to establish rules to spare himself the harder work of personally interacting with and discipling a young person. Not all rules are created for this purpose, but it is possible for a shepherd to build high fences simply to make shepherding easy. This overemphasis on fences can provide justification for the errant sheep to follow wrong desires. A carnal-minded church member can feel better about straying if he is reacting to a leader who is not modeling the Good Shepherd.

"That the World May Know"

God expects his church to operate in love—love that patiently waits, suffers with strugglers, and willingly gives up personal desires for the good of the vision. This is much different than ignoring or tolerating our differences. The church is called to exhibit self-denying love in pursuit of God's greater purpose. I am asked to lay down my rights and lovingly seek the good of my brother.

What about your church? Are you concerned about unity, or have you just learned to tolerate each other? And beyond unity, are you operating in love? It is one thing to have visible cohesion. The military does that. It is another thing entirely to do this in love, and it is this strong, visible love between members that will point the seeker to Christ.

Are you able to come together, prayerfully consider the Scriptures, and then lovingly agree on a united way to apply them in daily life? And if you are able to do this, is your focus only on yourselves, your families, and the future of your congregation? Or have you also seriously considered and embraced Jesus' vision and purpose for unity: "that the world may know"?[j]

---

[j] John 17:23

CHAPTER TWENTY-ONE

The Devastation of Divorce

None of us can fully comprehend the incredible consequences of divorce. How do you quantify the emotional pain, financial loss, and damage to children? According to a 2014 report by Pew Research,[1] only 46 percent of American children younger than eighteen were living in a home with a traditional father and mother in their first marriage. This is an alarming change! In 1980, 61 percent fit this description, and in 1970, 73 percent of American children lived in traditional homes. Returning to an empty house is now normal for the majority of children. While we might expect this tragedy to exist in a secular society, it is extremely disheartening to hear of so many dysfunctional homes and such high divorce rates among professing Christians.[2] After all, marriage is intended to reveal a very precious truth to the world.

The Apostle Paul wrote to the church at Ephesus that a husband's love for his wife is to reflect Christ's love for the church, and a wife's submission to her husband is to demonstrate the church's obedience to Christ.[a] A godly marriage is intended to provide a living example

---

[a] Ephesians 5:22–33

of the great love and vibrant relationship between Christ and His church. A healthy marriage is not just about two people getting along and avoiding conflict. It should demonstrate Christ's sacrificial love for His church and the church's submission to Christ. God is depending on our marriages to exhibit the greatness and glory of God Himself!

So what happens when marriages become dysfunctional? The image of God is marred and distorted. The beautiful light that was intended to shine into a dark world becomes dimmed, and observers get an inaccurate picture of God's glory and character. Divorce distorts God's illustration of His love.

The same is true when divorce occurs in churches.

Divorce in the Brotherhood

Like believers committed in Christian marriage, God wants the local church to demonstrate the character and love of God. So what happens when tension, infighting, and cliques enter a brotherhood? It distorts Jesus' vision for His church.

Recently I spoke with a man who had been involved in a church plant in an isolated area. His family had moved there to reach out in the community, but after several years, tension developed and the church split. Today there are two churches in this small community. To an onlooker there is little difference. They have similar statements of faith and meet at the same time on Sunday mornings just a few miles apart. And even though each congregation can explain to neighbors why its doctrinal position is more Scripturally sound, neither has many seekers from the community. In fact, it is extremely rare for either to have visitors. I suspect they could preach powerful messages, hold revivals, conduct tent meetings, and even go door to door passing out tracts. They could put up a billboard telling their neighbors of the transforming power of Jesus. But the fact that they can't get along with each other shouts so loudly that their neighbors will have difficulty hearing the Gospel.

A church without sacrificial love is like an orchestra that can't harmonize. Members may have excellent instruments and be skillful players. They may even enjoy the fellowship of getting together, socializing, and playing. But if they can't harmonize, the crowds will be small and visitors few.

Let's go back to the Shady Oak congregation where Firmon Tradition and Neidmor Outreach separated due to conflict. Someone else was affected by this separation. His name is Sammy Seeker.

Sammy Seeker

Sammy wasn't raised in a godly home. His parents divorced when he was young, and his life was difficult. After marrying Sarah, a nice local girl, he focused on work, weekends, and paying the bills. But after a few years and a few children, Sammy and Sarah felt something was lacking. They had experienced conflicts in their marriage and difficulties with their children. They began to suspect they were missing an important ingredient in their lives.

Just down the road from Sammy and Sarah was a small community church, and one day a friendly member from this congregation dropped by to invite them to services. Sammy's family began to attend, and they soon realized that Jesus was what they had been missing. Sammy and Sarah committed their lives to the Lord and became faithful church members. They also began to study the Word of God at home and apply its teachings to their lives.

Several years went by before Sammy and Sarah made some disturbing discoveries. Their pastor seemed to disregard some basic teachings of Jesus. They read what Jesus said about loving their enemies[b] and were confused by their pastor's militaristic patriotism. They read

---

[b] Matthew 5:44

Jesus' words regarding divorce and remarriage[c] and were troubled. Their pastor, whom they dearly loved, was ignoring this basic command, and he didn't seem receptive to their concerns.

Finally, in exasperation, Sammy Seeker and his family began to search for another church. Sunday after Sunday found Sammy and Sarah visiting churches, looking for a group that was serious about following Jesus and obeying His teachings.

Months went by, and just when they were about to give up, they found Shady Oak. Neidmor Outreach met them at the door, and they were enthralled. This was exactly what they had been searching for! The members of Shady Oak were devoted to the Word of God and willing to live it out regardless of personal cost. But the cost of committing to the church was high, and some of the church's rules seemed inconsistent. For example, Sammy had always enjoyed playing golf, and he was told this would need to stop. It was a waste of money, and believers should focus on more edifying activities. But when hunting season came around, Sammy was shocked at the amount of time, money, and discussion that surrounded this sport. Some even took expensive hunting and fishing trips to other areas. All of this confused him. Furthermore, why was it acceptable to buy expensive vehicles as long as they were a particular color?

Sammy and Sarah stayed up late some nights wrestling with these kinds of questions. But in the end they decided the cost was worth it. Even though some things were still confusing, they had a deep desire to follow Jesus, and one year later they were faithful, committed members of the Shady Oak congregation.

Unknown to Sammy and Sarah, this group had some hidden fault lines. Shortly after joining the church, they began to see and hear things that disturbed them. At first they couldn't identify what it was, but they felt a certain tension in the air during some messages and discussions. Outwardly everyone seemed to love each other, but when Firmon

---

[c] Mark 10:11, 12

Tradition spoke on preserving what they had, some were uneasy. And when Neidmor Outreach stressed outreach during a message, there seemed to be a stirring among a different part of the congregation. All of this was disquieting to Sammy, especially when some members attempted to persuade him to see issues from their perspective.

Sammy and Sarah had come to Shady Oak because they wanted a closer walk with the Lord, a place where their family could be taught a better way. Shady Oak was an oasis in a dry land, a refuge from a self-focused culture. But as they watched the undercurrent of conflict, Sammy began to suspect the oasis he had seen was just a mirage. On Sunday mornings the congregation was all smiles. Everyone professed to love each other and always spoke well of each other in public. But privately it was different. These same people began to quietly inform Sammy of the weaknesses of other members, trying to convince him to join their side. Several times Sammy met with various members of the congregation, pleading with them to work things out. Didn't they realize what a valuable thing they had? Didn't they understand how much a lost world needed to see a group that loves one another?

As Sammy and Sarah watched the congregation's unity unravel, they began to have serious doubts. Was Shady Oak actually more committed to following Jesus than the church they had left? Which was more important, the correct view on divorce, or loving your brother? Not going to war, or being willing to work out conflicts in love as Jesus taught? Shady Oak might be more doctrinally correct, but without love it did not paint a nice picture. The ministers at Shady Oak were good at articulating the deficiencies of the modern evangelical church, but tragically, their lack of love exposed deficiencies of their own. They would be willing to sit in a prison cell

> We would be willing to sit in a prison cell rather than go to war, but have trouble sitting down and communicating in love as brothers.

rather than go to war, but they had trouble sitting down and communicating in love as brothers. They, like the community church, were very interested in following Jesus, but only in certain areas. Eventually, Sammy's family walked away, confused and frustrated.

Many of us can think of scenarios like this. Individuals come seeking something better and are initially sure they have found it. But eventually they decide that strife, division, and continual wrestling within the church are not worth it. It is wonderful to articulate good doctrines, but what benefit is good doctrine if a church lacks the love of Jesus that pulls people together?

Ten Years Later
Every day on his way to work, Sammy Seeker drove past the Shady Oak building. Often he looked in and pondered the past. At one time he had been sure those people had what his family needed. They were nice people, and he certainly missed their good cooking. But he could still remember hurtful statements some of them had made about others in the congregation. After the church divided, he had visited both groups. After all, he had good friends on both sides. But after a few months he had given up. His children had overheard disparaging comments from other children about members in the other group, and Sammy had not been sure how to answer the questions this raised. These were people who claimed to follow Jesus, yet when things got tense, they responded like the unbelievers he worked with every day.

"Of the Same Mind"
The Apostle Paul, writing to the church at Philippi, repeatedly gives a plea for unity. "Fulfil ye my joy, that ye be likeminded, having the same love, being of one accord, of one mind."[d] And, "Nevertheless, whereto we have already attained, let us walk by the same rule, let us mind the same thing."[e]

At the end of the letter he gets even more specific, naming two

---

[d] Philippians 2:2
[e] Philippians 3:16

women involved in conflict. "I beseech Euodias, and beseech Syntyche, that they be of the same mind in the Lord."[f]

How do two women who see things differently become "of the same mind"? What does that even mean? Does each need to find out how the other one thinks and start thinking that way? And if so, which one sets the standard?

I don't believe Paul was saying they all needed to see life the same. To do so would result in a tremendous loss of power. But I do believe he was saying they needed to have a single goal and a unifying vision.

Consider marriage once more. Does a successful marriage depend on a husband and wife viewing every situation exactly alike? Of course not. But if they are going to have a prosperous relationship, each will need to have more regard for the relationship than for his or her own personal desires. This same principle applies in our churches. Churches will experience peace when each member places higher value on the unity of the group than on being right. When every member is willing to lay down his will for the good of the group, there will be unity.

These statements, however, must be considered in light of other truths. Unity is not the only important thing in a church. Looking back at the state church leading up to the Reformation, we see a well-oiled machine that claimed to be the church of God, yet bore little resemblance to the early church. Like an orchestra gone rogue, they were industriously producing loud music, but totally ignoring God's tune. Not only were they off key, they were playing the wrong song! A church can be orderly, unified, and walking in lockstep with each other, yet be far from God's vision.

---

[f] Philippians 4:2

CHAPTER TWENTY-TWO

Grounds for Divorce?

For some time I have been asking people from a variety of conservative fellowships a couple of questions. First, "Under what conditions, other than obvious doctrinal washout, should a person leave his church?"

The answers have been interesting. I have listened to long meandering responses, and most people are reluctant to draw a definite line. All agree that a person should walk away from a fellowship if Biblical truth is ignored, but how much doctrinal error is to be overlooked? What if one feels called to "strengthen the things which remain, that are ready to die?"[a] Several referenced the age of children and how the local church environment might be impacting their lives. Even if their church drifted in an undesirable path, they would be willing to stay longer if their children were older and more firmly grounded in their beliefs.

I also asked another question. "As you observe people moving their membership from one fellowship to another, would you say

---

[a] Revelation 3:2

it is usually for doctrinal reasons, concern for their families, or simply a desire for less restriction?" These answers have been more alarming. Most said very few are transferring their membership over important doctrinal teachings or differences in statements of faith. In reality, many of these churches have stated doctrinal beliefs that are almost identical.

So why are people swapping fellowships? As I listened, two main reasons surfaced. First, some are weary of restrictions. They desire more personal liberty and are tired of being told what to do.

Others change because of a deep-seated desire for a closer walk with God, a better environment for their children, and a closer, more vibrant brotherhood. They sense deadness in their church and are looking for life.

It is very difficult to determine true motives because both groups of people give the same reasons for leaving. They just want to get back to the Bible!

Back to the Bible

I interviewed one man I'll call Steven. He had left a fellowship years before when he felt it had become apathetic. The statement of faith was sound, the congregation was full of nice people, and he viewed the leadership as godly men. But the fire was gone, and Steven was fearful of raising his children in a listless, sleepy church environment. As he looks back, he is thankful he made the change and believes it has blessed his family. What amazes him is the path of many others who left at the same time. Steven clearly remembers a brother holding up a Bible during a discussion and stating emphatically, "We need to get back to the Bible!" At the time, Steven agreed completely and felt they were on the same page. But as the years have passed, he has come to realize things were not quite what they had seemed to be. Today the man who held up the Bible has drifted far from Biblical truth. After leaving that church, he merged into culture and eventually walked away from God.

Jeremiah said a long time ago, "The heart is deceitful above all things, and desperately wicked: who can know it?"[b] I suspect that many who see flaws, spiritual deadness, and lack of vibrancy in their local churches are correct in their assessment. These problems do exist. But these issues can also blind us to our own deficiencies. I can easily hide my love for the world behind faults I discover in my church. A leader in a church that has left its first love can become enamored with position or absorbed in maintaining the status quo. All of this can blind him to the reality that God is calling his congregation to higher ground.

How Should Separation Occur?
Separation within the church will happen. There were disagreements in the book of Acts, and there continue to be differences of opinion today. So how should these separations occur? In his book *I Will Build My Church*, Val Yoder provides an interesting insight.

> Matthew 18 tells us to first go alone and implore the erring brother to repent from his error. The same is true for the church member who detects doctrinal error in his church. He needs to first go alone to the local overseer after his own spirit has been molded and broken by prayer, fasting, and victoriously conquering the self-seeking spirit of independence that so often accompanies these confrontations.[1]

Most of us have grown up listening to Jesus' teaching regarding personal offenses. We have been taught to approach an erring brother with respect, humility, and an understanding that we may be the ones in error. We have been taught to have patience, to meet the brother alone, and to avoid the temptation to persuade others that our point of view is correct. I wonder how many church conflicts could be circumvented if disgruntled members

---

[b] Jeremiah 17:9

would follow this path before leaving. How many church divisions could be avoided simply by applying the principles laid out by Jesus Himself? But for this to occur, several important points should be considered.

Perhaps you are a father, concerned about the direction of your congregation and the future of your children. Maybe you are a young man extremely troubled by the lack of interest in evangelism. Are you willing to patiently and respectfully approach leadership, present your concerns, and allow time for them to prayerfully consider your point of view? Have you considered that your perspective might be incomplete and that your leadership might have experience you lack?

If you are a leader with members longing for reform, are you approachable? Have you retained the teachable spirit you possessed when ordained? Have you considered that the young man calling for more spiritual vibrancy might be speaking God's heart? Are you willing to admit that your perspective might not be complete? If God is calling your congregation to make some changes, do you really want to know?

One sincere young man spoke of approaching his bishop with concerns. At first the bishop listened patiently, but since that initial discussion, a wall has gone up. His leader no longer seems interested in him or his thoughts, and the young man is perplexed. What should he do now? He still carries this burden for the weak spiritual life in his church, but his bishop doesn't want to talk about it and seems to have little real interest in his concerns. This bishop seems to feel he has nothing to learn.

Impatient and idealistic youth, carnality among the members, leaders whose style of administration more closely resembles a business owner than a shepherd—these factors all contribute to dysfunction and division in churches. But something else is influencing us as well.

Lack of Commitment

The Apostle Paul, sitting in a Roman prison cell and writing to Timothy in Ephesus, made this spot-on prediction: "This know also, that in the last days perilous times shall come. For men shall be lovers of their own selves."[c] Self-love is the hallmark of our age. Some would say that our Western civilization is the most narcissistic and individualistic culture in recorded history. Consequently, we tend to resist commitments that tie us down. This lack of willingness to commit to others has a detrimental impact on our governments, businesses, and marriages.

And on our churches.

It is easy for me to read the words, "lovers of their own selves," and think of others. "Till death do us part" no longer means much, and I consider people who divorce and move on to be self-centered. However, if my commitment to my local brothers and sisters is only as deep as their willingness to embrace my opinion and provide for my needs, how much different is this than our culture's commitment to marriage? An unwillingness to make a long-term commitment to a local body of believers is one of our problems. This lack of commitment is devastating to Christ's vision for His body to live out loving unity "that the world may believe."

"Strengthen the Things That Remain"

Jesus sent letters, through the Apostle John, to seven of the churches in Asia. Addressing the believers at Sardis, Jesus had some difficult things to say. They were evidently a lifeless church, and Jesus said there were only a few who had "not defiled their garments."[d] Startling words! Just a few people left in the church who were faithfully following Jesus! But what I find most amazing is not what Jesus said to these faithful few, but what He didn't say. Jesus told them to "be watchful, and strengthen the things which remain, that are ready

---

[c] 2 Timothy 3:1, 2
[d] Revelation 3:4

to die,"ᵉ but He said nothing about moving to a different church. The very next church Jesus addresses is Philadelphia, and it must have been a thriving fellowship of on-fire believers. Even though this vibrant church appears to have been less than thirty miles down the road, there is no mention of swapping fellowships. Jesus' only instruction to the Sardis church was to get in and help build.

What do we learn from this? Should a person never change fellowships? Should he hang on as long as there are two or three believers? Maybe, but there is also a sober counter-balancing message in these letters. Jesus warned several of the churches that if something didn't change, He was going to come and do something about it. He warned one church that He would come quickly and fight against them,ᶠ told another He would come as a thief,ᵍ and warned another that He would spew them out of His mouth.ʰ Obviously, Jesus isn't pleased with people claiming to represent Him while teaching, living, and holding attitudes contrary to His will.

Notice what He said to the church at Ephesus: "Repent, and do the first works; or else I will come unto thee quickly, and will remove thy candlestick out of his place."ⁱ This church had once possessed a fervent love, but had left it. They had been a good witness, but their light was getting dim. If they didn't make some changes, Jesus was going to come and extinguish what little light they had left.

Do you suppose a church whose candlestick has been removed is aware of it? Or are there churches out there that still have services every Sunday, form committees, organize potlucks, and have good attendance, yet their candlestick has been removed? How long could inertia and organizational structure keep a church in operation? And if this fellowship exists, outwardly going through the motions but lacking the power of God, would you want to be a part of it?

ᵉ Revelation 3:2
ᶠ Revelation 2:16
ᵍ Revelation 3:3
ʰ Revelation 3:16
ⁱ Revelation 2:5

There is a time to leave a fellowship, and sometimes that decision is forced upon us. However, choosing to divide a church or leave a fellowship should occur only after every possible path of reconciliation has been pursued. If you are in a situation where ecclesiastical divorce seems inevitable, are you actively working toward reviving what remains? It will require prayer, fasting, and a deep desire to demonstrate something beautiful to the world. It will also require commitment to the local body and the purpose Christ has for His church. Remember, we have a God who loves to breathe new life into impossible situations.

My wife and I have been married for many years, but we have not enjoyed a happy marriage just because we each found a compatible spouse. Those who know us well would tell you that in many ways we are very incompatible. Our personalities are different, we enjoy different activities, and we even like different foods. I have many flaws she deals with daily. (She could enumerate them if you had time to listen.) Yet we are still together because we value our marriage above our own personal desires. We are both willing to sacrifice our wants to make our marriage successful.

Consider your relationship with your church. Are you known as people who love each other so deeply that you are willing to overlook flaws and differences in personalities? Let me describe your church. You have people with different gifts and different temperaments, some of whom are very difficult to get along with. The Lord wouldn't let you escape without some of those! The marvel of God's vision for His church is this: He expects you to take these imperfect ingredients and become one in Him. There is both power and purpose in oneness. The power to accomplish this must come from Him, and the purpose is simple. God's desire is for His church to produce beautiful, harmonious, and compelling music for a dying world.

PART SIX

What Is GOD'S Vision?

CHAPTER TWENTY-THREE

How Big Is Your Vision?

As he reached altitude, leveled off, sat back in his seat, and nosed his plane along the beautiful Monterey coast toward Oakland, California, Gary Kildall must have marveled at how good life had been to him. It was July 1980, and at thirty-eight years old he was already a very wealthy man. Gary was the owner of Digital Research, Inc. (DRI), which produced a computer operating system known as CPM. He had built this operating system on his own in a tool shed behind his home, and it had caught on quickly. With the computer age taking off like a rocket, CPM was the industry standard, and the future couldn't have looked brighter.

Growing up in Seattle with his father working as a sea captain, there was nothing to indicate wealth or greatness in Gary's future. With a degree from the University of Washington, he became a mathematics teacher and developed an interest in computer technology. At the time, the computer industry was focused on big business, military projects, and organizations like NASA that needed to crunch huge masses of data.

Since every computer needs an operating system and his company was the recognized front-runner, Gary Kildall had every reason to smile that morning. He was at the pinnacle of his career, his company was growing rapidly, and no competition even came close.

International Business Systems (IBM) was a leader in computer development at that time and had just started to develop a desktop computer. This was a novel idea. The only use for computers to date was for large organizations, and the thought of building a useful computer small enough to fit on a desk seemed strange. But IBM was developing an experimental model. Needing an operating system, they had contacted Gary's company. They wanted the very best, and Digital Research was the obvious choice. As Gary flew toward Oakland, he knew IBM would be visiting his company that day. But why should he stay at home and talk to them? After all, what options did IBM really have? His operating system was the best available, and he wasn't going to stay at home just for them. He would discuss this issue when it was convenient for him. The day that began so beautifully became a day Gary Kildall would regret till he died.

When IBM arrived at Digital Research's office and found no one there to talk to, they began to consider other options. CPM was the best out there, but couldn't another operating system be developed for desktops? Surely someone else would be easier to work with and could design a system specifically to fit their needs. They began to search, and one month later discovered a little-known programmer in Seattle who was willing to work with them: Bill Gates. He was only twenty-four years old at the time, and the company he and a couple other programmers had just started was called Microsoft. Today, few people have even heard of Digital Research, which went out of business in 1991. But almost everyone on the globe knows about Microsoft, and it all goes back to a day in July 1980 when

Gary Kildall underestimated the potential of personal computing.[1]

I believe many of our problems with church are similar. We have underestimated the power of church, and our vision is far too small.

Church: The Powerful Potential

We like to read those first few chapters in the book of Acts. It was an extraordinary time to be alive, yet it wasn't easy. Place yourself in the apostles' situation for a moment and think of all the things they lacked. They didn't have Bibles as we know them today, they lacked experience, and they had little idea how a church was to operate. Those first few years were tumultuous. New people were coming to faith from all kinds of cultures, languages, and heathen beliefs. The church had blatant sin, false brethren within, and fierce opposition without. Consequently, there was little stability in those first few years. So much of it was exactly what we don't want in church life. So why do we enjoy reading the book of Acts? What was different about those early believers?

There are many answers to this question, but I believe one difference is this: they saw religious opposition, the world, and the power of Satan as conquered and ineffective. They saw Jesus and His church as powerful, mighty, and having the potential to overcome. Christ had given them great power, and they weren't about to miss this terrific opportunity. They saw the church as big and the world as small.

> They saw the church as big and the world as small.

Looking around today, it seems like we have it upside down. We have church divisions, internal conflicts, struggling youth, and congregations drifting listlessly closer to the world. Discouraging news regarding our churches has become normal, while the daily paper brings fresh reports that the powers of darkness are increasing—random shootings, gay marriage, and a moral code unraveling at an astounding pace. We wonder how long things can go on. The world seems big and powerful and the church small and ineffective.

Have you ever wondered if the present-day church has drifted so far that those early believers wouldn't even recognize it? While modern denominations have been formed out of reaction to error, the early church wasn't. It wasn't even built around some godly man. It was simply the Holy Spirit breathing the heart, power, and vision of God into ordinary men and women. The early church wasn't flawless. We have many letters written to struggling churches to prove that. We don't need to read very far in the epistles to discover that we can identify with their difficulties.

The book of Acts was given as a model, an opportunity for us to learn and visualize what God had in mind. If my church bears little resemblance to God's idea of a church, it is time for me to stop and rethink my church vision. God has not worked precisely the same in every age, and our set of circumstances will not exactly mirror the time of the early church. God moved in some amazing ways then that have never been replicated since. However, the basic principles in that early church should be evident in every vibrant church today.

Two overviews of the early church are found at the end of Acts 2 and 4, and I would encourage you to read these passages often. Keep God's purpose in mind, and let the early church polish your vision. Let's look as some basic timeless principles in the book of Acts that should be part of our vision today.

Prayer and Fasting
There is a clear underlying reliance on God throughout the book of Acts. These were not strong, self-assured men striding around proclaiming a message solely based on their own power or experience. One gets the impression of men who knew their inability and need of constant infilling of the Holy Spirit. Notice these words as they gathered after being threatened by the authorities: "And being let go, they went to their own company, and reported all that the chief

priests and elders had said unto them. And when they heard that, they lifted up their voice to God with one accord."[a]

Try to visualize what this might have looked and sounded like. What would it have sounded like to have a room full of people raising their voices with one accord? Emotional? Disorderly? But don't miss the passion in the description. These people were not just praying because it was time to pray and praying is what good Christians do. They came with a posture of, "We have a major problem, and we don't have the answers!" Later in Acts, on several occasions, we see them collectively praying and fasting. They knew their need was great. As you consider a vision for church, be sure that it includes frequent calls for prayer and fasting. We underestimate our need, and our churches today should be known as groups of people who understand their desperate need for God Himself.

> Our churches today should be known as groups of people who understand their desperate need for God Himself.

"One Heart and One Soul"

"And the multitude of them that believed were of one heart and of one soul."[b] You can't read the book of Acts without seeing a cohesive love and unity among those first followers of Jesus. We see phrases like "of one accord," "they were together," and "they were of one heart and one soul." This is even more astonishing as we realize that they were coming from different cultures, social strata, and financial standings. They were so focused on Jesus Christ that all those other distinguishing issues seemed inconsequential. Former murderers sat beside bankers, and former beggars communed with

---

[a] Acts 4:23, 24
[b] Acts 4:32

wealthy merchants. It must have been incredible! Those looking on must have marveled at their love! They had never seen anything like this before.

A Vision Larger Than Themselves

Chased from city to city, threatened with prison, and martyred for their faith—if ever believers deserved some peace and quiet, surely it was those in the book of Acts. But notice the focus of their prayer after their first taste of persecution. "And now, Lord, behold their threatenings: and grant unto thy servants, that with all boldness they may speak thy word."[c]

Imagine that your congregation has just been told by the authorities to quiet down. "Go ahead and live your lives, but don't tell others about this Jesus." How would your church deal with this? What would be the focus of your prayers the next Sunday? For protection? That you might get back to living a quiet and enjoyable life?

I find it amazing that there is no request in this prayer for their own safety. They were not reminding God that they were in trouble and needed their leaders. There were no petitions about avoiding martyrdom. None! Their only focus seemed to be sharing the kingdom of Jesus Christ with others. It was a marvelous time, but before we decide it was just different then, let's be sure we are sensing the heart of God and incorporating this principle into our church vision. The early church had a purpose much greater than themselves, and so should we.

Signs and Wonders

One feature about the early church that stands out to us in the Western world is the miracles that were performed. The second chapter of Acts sums it up like this: "And fear came upon every soul: and many wonders and signs were done by the apostles."[d] Jesus had healed people, and the apostles were simply following in His steps.

---

[c] Acts 4:29
[d] Acts 2:43

But as we follow on through the book of Acts, and then into the early church writings, there seems to be a decreasing focus on miracles. Today, as you travel around the world, miraculous healings still happen. But you will find them occurring with much greater frequency in areas of extreme poverty and where Bibles are scarce. I have talked to church leaders in restricted countries who have seen many miracles, yet I have also been intrigued with their lack of preoccupation with the miraculous. They are willing to share their marvelous stories, but what they would really like is more Bibles and sound teaching.

Let's not exclude signs and wonders in our vision for a church. We don't know what is on the horizon, and as our culture continues to move away from God, He may once again exhibit His great power through signs and wonders. We tend to develop ideologies and doctrines over time that correspond to our experience, but let's allow God to be God. If He chooses to increase His use of miracles to expand His kingdom, even right here in America, let's be open to it.

Their Possessions Were Affected

Following Jesus had a powerful impact on the early Christians' money and possessions, but a word of caution is in order here. I have heard many discussions about that first church in Jerusalem and what it means to have "all things in common."[e] Some push for communal living, wondering why people can't just take the Bible literally. Then someone else pushes back, pointing to verses in Timothy[f] that speak of wealthy individuals within the church, and passages in Corinthians[g] that encourage personal giving and seem to contradict the concept of living out of one purse. We walk away from these arguments, each side more entrenched in its way of thinking and neither seriously considering how the basic principle displayed by the early church should affect their lives.

---

[e] Acts 2:44
[f] 1 Timothy 6:17, 18
[g] 2 Corinthians 8 & 9

Let's admit there are different ways to live out some of Jesus' teachings; then, let's focus on encouraging each other to move toward the underlying principle. Otherwise, we may get so caught up in arguing that we fail to apply what we know. Debate is easy to hide behind and can help us avoid making conscious choices to follow Jesus in practical ways. Make no mistake. When a congregation returns to the vision of the early church, *their possessions will be affected.*

We struggle to grasp the reality that our vision for church is too small. Gary Kildall underestimated the potential in desktop computers. He had all the resources he needed at his fingertips, but he missed a tremendous opportunity, hindered only by self-satisfaction and complacency.

I suggest the church today is hampered by the same. We are handicapped, not because of a darkening society, loose morals, or because Satan's empire is growing in strength. Rather, we have underestimated the power of God and the great potential in vibrant communities collectively living out the teachings of Jesus in daily life. Our vision has been too small!

CHAPTER TWENTY-FOUR

Strong versus Weak Churches

While traveling in a developing country, I attended a small Anabaptist church on a Sunday morning. It was a simple building with a bare concrete floor and a tin roof, but the service itself impressed me. This little church, with less than twenty-five members, had two ordained leaders, but both had been called away to neighboring communities and were preaching in churches even smaller than this one. So men from the congregation led the service.

I could not understand the language and there was no interpreter, but I can still see the man standing there preaching. He didn't have a dynamic delivery, but he had a smile on his face and a joyful message. I knew why. Just several years earlier this man had been known in the community as a drunk, a woman chaser, and a murderer. Then he had found redemption through the blood of Jesus, and he enjoyed re-telling the story of the cross. Sitting across the aisle were his wife and children. This man's wife could have told many sordid stories of past struggle and betrayal, but her contented smile told more than words could ever express.

I had visited this church before and knew these people's

circumstances. My eyes scanned the people sitting in front of me, and all of them had rocky pasts. In fact, only one person could have been considered a stable believer for many years. Leaving the service that day, a couple of questions kept circling through my mind. Was that a strong church or a weak one? And what are the criteria for a strong church?

Years ago when I visited a house church in China, a nineteen-year-old girl told me she had been a believer longer than anyone else in her church. They were pleading for more teaching. They knew they were a weak church and were hoping a strong church from America would send a leader who could give them sound Biblical instruction. But was that really a weak church? Is a church that is keenly aware of its own deficiency actually ineffective? I know of churches that have hundreds of members, steady leadership, and predictable services. Year after year goes by and little seems to change. These are stable churches, but are they strong ones?

"When I Am Weak . . ."

The Apostle Paul told the church at Corinth how he had prayed earnestly for the removal of the thorn in his flesh. God had responded by saying, "My grace is sufficient for thee: for my strength is made perfect in weakness." Paul then says, "Most gladly therefore will I rather glory in my infirmities, that the power of Christ may rest upon me. Therefore I take pleasure in infirmities, in reproaches, in necessities, in persecutions, in distresses for Christ's sake: for when I am weak, then am I strong."[a]

---

[a] 2 Corinthians 12:9, 10

The times Paul felt he was strong and had his spiritual house in order were the very times of greatest risk. The times when he felt spiritually weak were the times he was actually strong. What a paradox! Most of us have discovered that it is in times of weakness that we cry out to the Lord. The path ahead looks impossible and options are few, so we turn to God and find the strength to meet the challenge. Could this same principle apply to our churches? Is it possible that our greatest danger lies in believing our church is strong and unshakable?

Dodder Weed

I was working in my office one morning when my daughter came in. "Daddy, you need to come look at this weed in our flowerbed. It is really spreading, and something needs to be done about it."

I was busy and didn't think I had time to mess with flowerbeds, so without looking up I gave a quick response. "I'll spray it with Roundup the next time I spray."

"I tried that. I don't think Roundup will kill this kind of weed."

Now she had my attention. I don't have much extra time to spend in flowerbeds, and Roundup is my army of one. If Roundup won't kill it, I have a problem. Walking with my daughter to the flowerbed, I saw a weed I had not known existed. After some research I finally discovered its name is *Cuscuta,* or dodder weed. Dodder weed is in the morning glory family, a parasitic plant, usually yellow in color.

Dodder seeds germinate near the surface of the soil, and as soon as the sprout emerges, the tiny plant immediately begins to search for a host plant. Using time-lapse photography, researchers have sped up videos to show how this tiny sprout finds its source of nourishment. As it grows, the tiny yellow shoot circles, reaching out as far as possible in a frantic search for a healthy plant to attach to. It is a desperate pursuit, for if the dodder weed has not successfully attached itself to a host plant within five to ten days, it will die. As soon as the dodder attaches itself to another plant, its roots begin to die. There may be healthy soil just below it, but once it connects to the sap of another plant, all the soil nutrients are ignored, and the dodder weed draws its life from the energy of its host plant.

Earlier we looked at the power and purpose of oneness and unity within a church, but there is a corresponding danger we must not overlook. Seeking God, pursuing His will, meditating on His words, and engaging in fasting and prayer is hard work. Like the dodder weed, it is very easy to attach myself to others and trust in the fact that I am connected to a strong group. Why go through all the struggle of pursuing a close personal connection with God? It is so much easier to draw life from the group. Why push roots down into rocky soil when I can connect to a community that looks good, that can explain why it is better than others, and that promises to provide what I need? We need to understand the great danger here. It is possible for an entire community to do this, everyone getting life from everyone else and feeling good about the level of spirituality without individuals personally being rooted in God.

I wonder if this was part of the problem with the church at Laodicea. They were well fed, liked how things were going, and felt they had a strong church. But notice Jesus' words: "Because thou sayest, I am rich, and increased with goods, and have need of nothing; and knowest not that thou art wretched, and miserable, and poor, and blind, and naked . . ."[b]

I think this church was shocked by this message. They may have even suspected that this letter got in the wrong mailbox! What could he mean, saying they were wretched, miserable, poor, blind, and naked? Didn't they have a full house every Lord's Day and a full treasury? And there was no church around with better preaching!

But something was missing. As I read the letter to Laodicea, I can't help but wonder how many of them were intentionally pursuing God in the quietness of their own hearts and closets. Were they

---

[b] Revelation 3:17

possibly rejoicing in their unity, yet ignoring the one relationship that was truly essential? Jesus finishes this letter with tender words. Notice the patient and loving call of a God who still desires personal connection. "Behold, I stand at the door, and knock: if any man hear my voice, and open the door, I will come in to him, and will sup with him, and he with me."[c]

Here were believers who were confident in their strength, yet God said they were weak. Despite His harsh assessment, Jesus didn't throw them out. He continued to plead with them, and I believe He is doing the same with our churches today. If we will simply repent of our egocentric attitudes and turn back to Him, He is eager to bless.

The Strength in Weak Churches

The little church I described at the beginning of this chapter knows it is weak. Those who attend are under no illusion that just drawing energy from each other will be enough. If they are going to survive, every member will need intimate connection with Jesus Christ. That is the inherent strength in churches that know their weaknesses.

One of the questions I hear discussed frequently in larger, stable churches is, "How can we help everyone feel needed?" Leaders are rightly concerned about the brother who sits in row fourteen every Sunday. He's always there, but they wish for some way to get him more involved. So they create jobs, start programs, and the primary goal seems to be that everyone feels included. Over time the church's goal becomes keeping everyone busy and feeling fulfilled. This is quite different from what we see in Acts.

Can you imagine the apostles sitting down and discussing how to make everyone feel included? "I've been noticing Barnabas is getting a little restless. Isn't there a job we could give him so he feels fulfilled?" Or, "Have you noticed Luke lately? He's starting to look a little bored. Isn't there something we could have him do so he feels included?"

Preposterous! In the heat of battle, army generals do not meet

---

[c] Revelation 3:20

to make sure everyone feels involved. When this occurs in our churches, a red flag should instantly go up—something is dreadfully wrong with our church vision. When a church is healthy and fully engaged in the battle, no one needs to worry about people feeling involved.

> When a church is healthy and fully engaged in the battle, no one needs to worry about people feeling involved.

Creating Codependency

Sometimes an unhealthy emotional or psychological reliance exists between people. Counselors call this codependency, and this can develop in many ways. Perhaps a mother has an older wayward child. He should be getting a job, but things just never quite work out, and rather than letting her son experience the consequences of no income, she tries to help. Occasionally she slips him a little money, and an unhealthy cycle develops. He's not learning from his mistakes, and she enjoys feeling needed. This is codependency.

Codependency can thrive in churches as well. A few godly and overworked leaders rush from meeting to meeting, trying to meet the demands of the congregation. Pastor John breathlessly heads over to see Brother Joe, who has been involved in an ongoing interpersonal conflict. Then it's back home to get his wife before heading to Sister Susie's house and spending an hour listening to her woes and praying with her. The next night there is a meeting of church leaders to plan a family retreat, and then a couple of phone calls before bed from disgruntled members. Pastor John rushes from meeting to meeting, and sometimes he wonders, *Is this really what God had in mind?* But he quickly squelches his doubts. *I have been called to lead and shouldn't complain if it isn't easy. I am just glad for this opportunity to serve the Lord!* And in this way Pastor John finds his fulfillment in meeting the many needs of his congregation.

In the same congregation, Ron sits at home reading the news. Scanning over the newspaper, he marvels at how fast grain prices have dropped. He reaches for more popcorn and shakes his head. Ten percent drop in less than a month! He is glad he doesn't farm. He likes to spend his Saturdays fishing or getting things done around the house. Ron's a strong supporter of his congregation and is glad he belongs to a good church with such godly and dependable leaders. There have been times, though, when Ron has wondered, *Is mowing the church lawn and being obedient all there is to Christianity?* Even though John and Ron are in the same church, their church life is totally different. While one scarcely has time to fulfill his tasks, the other senses he should be doing more.

The New Testament shows the importance of leadership in the church, but when the church turns inward and its main purpose is to make everyone feel included, codependency seems inevitable. When churches are alive, have a vision beyond themselves, and are purposely engaged in the battle, the problem of codependency will disappear for one simple reason: every member is actually needed! One Chinese pastor describes the task of a leader like this: "A church is meant to be a training center and command hub for war, not a social hub for pleasantries and hypocrisy, where people give lip service to Christ while refusing to obey His commands."[1] A leader is not called to do all the work. Rather, he is called to prepare and inspire his people to work.

Strong or Weak?

The truth is, all of our churches are weak. We all need the power of God to be effective in warfare. When we decide that stability, peace, and continuity are equivalent to strength, we are at great risk. An effective church is one in which every member is needed in the battle and feels his dependence on the Lord Jesus. Just as every groom likes to care for and provide for his bride, our Lord Jesus wants to provide and care for us. I can think of few things more disappointing to a groom than to discover that his bride is self-absorbed and has no need of him.

CHAPTER TWENTY-FIVE

The Christian Community Commitment

Benedict was raised in wealth, the son of a Roman noble. He had left his home in Nursia, a small village in central Italy, to visit the city of Rome. Upon arriving, he was shocked at its decay. Rome was no longer a glorious city of power and prestige. It had been sacked years before and was a pathetic shadow of its former self. As Benedict surveyed the moral landscape near the turn of the sixth century, he concluded that his only option was to withdraw from society and serve the Lord in the wilderness.

Benedict lived alone in a cave outside of Rome for several years, but eventually others with a desire to follow God sought him out. During his life Benedict founded twelve monasteries in this region. Looking back from our vantage point, Benedict did more than just withdraw. He lived out and taught the concept of Christian community.

After the fall of Rome, Europe experienced tremendous upheaval. Poverty was rampant, barbarous tribal conflicts flared up, and chaos reigned. The trade network Rome had developed fell apart, and the structured social life Europe had enjoyed disintegrated. During these years Benedict's communities continued to teach the people how to read, plant crops, and build. They evangelized the common people and taught them how to pray. These communities maintained the seeds needed for a civilization to flourish over the next few centuries. Modern historians look back and say that Benedict's communities preserved what was good in post-Roman Europe, helping the region to eventually recover.

Today there is a resurgence of interest in this movement. Despite the modern evangelical foray into politics and social activism, the American moral slide continues. Some within the larger Christian world are, like Benedict, wondering if focusing on building Christian communities is a better approach than using a political platform. In 2017 the book *The Benedict Option* hit American bookshelves and was an immediate success. But why would citizens in a country known for promoting independence and self-centeredness become enthralled with a book about the beauty of community?

Americans know something is missing. They are filling their lives with sports, entertainment, and social media. Yet in the midst of this, they feel empty. Rod Dreher in *The Benedict Option* says, "As the West declines into spiritual acedia [apathy], there will be more and more people who are seeking something real, something meaningful, and yes, something wholesome. It is our mandate as Christians to give it to them."[1]

Western civilization, like post-Roman Europe, is in trouble. The Apostle Paul told Timothy that "perilous times shall come,"[a] and we are seeing the fulfillment of that prophecy. Are we only capable of telling the world what is wrong, or can we exhibit something different? Can we only point out what is ugly, or can we show seekers something beautiful?

I believe our call today is to demonstrate love, beauty, and human flourishing in the face of hatred, evil, and human depravity. And I

---

[a] 2 Timothy 3:1

> Our call today is to demonstrate love, beauty, and human flourishing in the face of hatred, evil, and human depravity.

believe this is best accomplished through Christian community. Every human longs for meaningful relationship, purposeful interaction, and the security that comes from being interwoven with others. But what does it take to have community with others?

We commonly use this word in three ways. First, we use it to refer to a shared geographical location—a group of people who live in close proximity. They have a loyalty to each other simply because of where they live. They help each other, share tools, and watch out for each other when a storm hits. In my neighborhood, we have a variety of beliefs, income levels, and even languages. But we are neighbors geographically, and I am part of this community.

The second use of the word *community* refers to those with whom we share lifestyles or cultural heritage. We have neighbors who are part of the Basque community. The Basques are an ethnic group that originated in northeastern Spain and southwestern France, but today they are scattered all over the globe. Yet they have retained their identity, and wherever they find each other, they feel kinship. They value their language, teach their children their history, and make effort to preserve their customs. Because of their shared values, they are known as the Basque community.

Another type of community revolves around a group's focus—a sharing of purpose and goals. We see this type of community built around sports teams throughout the world. Fans may live in different areas and have totally different lifestyles, but there is a connection between people who root for the same team. I live in western America, yet have neighbors who are avid fans of teams thousands of miles away. They read about their teams, talk about the players, and wouldn't think of missing a game on television. These fans are bound together simply because they have a common loyalty to the purpose and goal of that team, and they willingly sacrifice time and money to maintain this allegiance.

Early Church Community

As we read about the lives of those first believers, it doesn't take long to realize that the early church shared all three types of community. When the writer of Acts says, "They had all things common,"[b] this commonality involved more than just finances. They shared geographical location, values, and goals. This doesn't mean there were no differences among them, but they were willing to blend their lives in a way that demonstrated the glory and power of God.

Attending versus Committing

Humans want connection. This is a powerful longing, even within the most hardened criminal. However, a second longing contradicts the first: we value personal independence. We don't want to submit to a group and have others tell us what to do. These two longings war within us.

Western culture and modern Christianity have tried to fulfill both of these desires by flaunting the idea that one can *belong* to the church without having to *commit* to it. Like a man who marries a wife while holding divorce as a possibility, we join churches knowing that we can always move on if things are not working how we want them to. We need to understand that attending services on Sunday mornings and Wednesday nights, giving financially, and serving on a few committees is much different than committing to a church community. It is obvious that those first followers of Jesus in the book of Acts were doing more than just belonging to a church. The church was not just a club of like-minded people. Rather, there was a deep love, loyalty, and commitment to each other. It was a family, and families take care of each other.

---

[b] Acts 2:44

Loss of Commitment

The differences between a church and a church community are significant, and in our culture there has been a slow drift away from commitment to community. This has impacted not only the church, but also the larger society, and secular sociologists are taking note. Recently, a major British news magazine published an article about the increase in deaths among middle-aged white American males. For years the mortality rate of this group had been dropping, but in the past twenty years it has shot up among those in this group who do not have a college degree. The article was called "Deaths of Despair," since this uptick in deaths has been due to alcohol abuse, drug overdose, and suicide. Notice what the author flags as one of the underlying reasons for this phenomenon: "As economic life has become less secure, low-skilled white men have tended toward unstable cohabiting relationships rather than marriages. They have abandoned traditional communal religion in favor of churches that emphasize personal identity."[2]

Commitment to relationships is essential to a society. When it is lost, chaos reigns. This is true whether we are talking about governments, marriages, or churches. So how do you know if you belong to a church or to a church community? One way to find out is to look at what happens when one of the members has a loss. When a man who belongs to a "church" dies, the local congregation will have a funeral, provide a nice meal, comfort his wife with cards and concern, and then move on. Almost every church out there will do this for a grieving widow.

When a man who is part of a "church community" dies, so much more occurs. The widow knows that she and her children will be cared for, whether the need is emotional or material. She belongs to a church family, and they are committed to her well-being. They will sacrifice to take care of her, sell property if needed, and make sure her family's needs are taken care of. This is what God intended, and this self-sacrificing love and care between believers is to be a public demonstration to a lost world. Loving church communities are God's way of reaching out to the lonely unbeliever.

The Problem

But what if the original purpose behind church community gets lost? What if a church turns inward, focusing on the security and treasure of community, but losing its concern for those outside the church? What if the single mom, the one just down the street trying desperately to hold down a low-paying job while raising several children, senses that she could never join your community? She looks on, and it looks so wonderful! Something within tells her it is the answer to those deep longings within her heart. Life looks discouraging, and she isn't sure it is worth continuing. She looks at your church and sees stable families, nice businesses, and well-mannered children. She knows she just wouldn't fit in. Besides, she is certain your church community is not really interested in the Mary Magdalenes of the neighborhood.

As I look around today, this is one of the saddest paradoxes of Christian community. Many of the groups who have retained the concept of commitment to community have lost interest in reaching out to a lost world. Conversely, the ones that have discounted or discarded the value of community are focusing on evangelism. Jesus said, "By this shall all men know that ye are my disciples, if ye have love one to another,"[c] and I believe it pains the heart of God to see His children ignore community on the one hand, or the purpose behind it on the other. It is still His desire that the world would see and believe.

> It pains the heart of God to see His children ignore community on the one hand, or the purpose behind it on the other.

---

[c] John 13:35

Blended Lives

Jesus' final prayer was that His followers may be made perfect in one, "that the world may know."[d] This is not going to happen by just meeting occasionally. Jesus was praying for more than gathering to listen to another sermon. He was calling for blended lives—communities of people all over the globe whose lives have been redeemed by Jesus and are now committed to Him and each other.

"Live and let live" is the mantra of our society, and many organizations promote tolerance. "Coexist" is the buzzword of religious and ideological tolerance. But the church of Jesus Christ is called to something much higher. We are called to self-denying love as we work in concert with those who have different gifts, pasts, and personalities. We are not called to just coexist in the church, but to lay down our own rights and desires for the good of the church community!

This is more than just people who are separate from society. Even ethnic minorities feel separate from mainstream culture. No, these believers are not focusing on the aspects of their lives that are different. Rather, they are focusing on Jesus Christ. The love they receive from Him flows out to each other, goes on to the hurting neighbor, and is observed by the unbelieving world. When lived out through the power of God and for His glory, it has the potential to turn the world upside down!

"That's Not My Church!"

Maybe you are thinking, *That sounds great, and I would love to be part of something like that, but that isn't my church. What am I supposed to do?* First, don't lose the passion for God's vision just because it isn't present reality. Blending lives, whether in marriage or in church community, is not easy. It takes patience, the power of God, and deep humility. As you desire to bring about reform, remember that God has chosen to reside and work within those possessing "a contrite and humble spirit."[e]

---

[d] John 17:23
[e] Isaiah 57:15

Many would-be reformers see the problem but lack the patience to wait on God and their church leadership. Sometimes it becomes evident that your church leaders really have no interest in pursuing both community and outreach. If this is where you are, spend time in prayer, communicate humbly with your leaders, and in time God will provide a path.

Second, be sure you are engaged in the battle while you wait. I have listened to many visionaries who assume that moving to a new community is the answer to their problem. But upon asking a few questions, it becomes evident that they are not fully engaged where they are. They may dream of going off to a foreign country where "real" outreach can take place, but they don't even know their neighbors and are making little contribution to their local congregation. This kind of dreaming is deadly to true spirituality. Dietrich Bonhoeffer gave this warning: "He who loves his dream of a community more than the Christian community itself becomes a destroyer of the latter, even though his personal intentions may be ever so honest and earnest and sacrificial."[3] It is so easy to hide an apathetic heart behind a lofty spiritual dream.

Is it possible God could use you right where you are, but your dream of a perfect church is keeping you from fully engaging with your community? Consider the thought in this poem, "The Vibrant Virtual Church":[f]

> It is so easy to hide an apathetic heart behind a lofty spiritual dream.

> The man loved to tell of a church with such life,
> That it never was bothered by gossip or strife.
> A place where each member shared blessing around,
> Words thoughtless or hurtful could never be found.

---

[f] By Gary Miller

This church, he told folks, loved the hurting and lost,
And a wandering sheep was sought at great cost.
In prisons and alleys where evil is crowned,
He'd seen them there freeing those Satan had bound.

When they met for service, each face had a glow,
Their harmonious singing was never too slow.
The preaching was powerful, the best he had heard,
The message was never by fear of man blurred.

He fruitlessly searched—for he had a mind keen—
For a church which compared to this church which he'd seen
Where sweet gentle children were kind when they played,
When one had a struggle, they all stopped and prayed.

He'd looked the world over, searched churches around,
Yet never an equal to this one he'd found.
Most churches have people who dabble with sin,
Their members all struggle again and again.

But this church, in contrast, had power within,
He had watched it for years and he'd never found sin.
So the man grew discouraged as he struggled to find
A church that compared to this church in his mind.

He loved to recount just how churches should be,
And he freely would try to help others see
How glorious and perfect if they, too, could find
This church that existed alone in his mind.

So from church to church he continually bounced,
As with zeal and great boldness he skillfully trounced
Each flaw that he found, and he freely maligned
Each church that was less than the one in his mind.

Many times we sit down and bemoan, and deplore,
While God has before us a wide open door.
But our minds are consumed by the fact that we find
That our church isn't quite like the one in our mind.

But I'm thankful, so glad, that our God didn't wait
And offer salvation to only the great.
T'was the feeble He died for, the halt and the blind;
It was imperfect people He had in His mind!

God has placed us in churches, imperfect and stressed,
Defective, deficient, lethargic at best.
But when God's our focus, with joy we will find,
More glorious His church, than the one in our mind!

God has not promised us perfect church communities. Just as personal sanctification is an ongoing process, so we find the process of building church communities. It is an ongoing work, and if we are going to pursue God's will in our churches, it will be both painful and rewarding.

You and Your Church?
As you consider the difference between attending a church and being committed to a church community, where are you? Do you just belong, or are you committed? Is there interest in more community, or are you comfortable with minimal involvement in each other's lives?

Perhaps you are part of a church that understands and lives out community, but has lost Jesus' original purpose. Maybe your group would rather not bother with the struggler down the road. Perhaps you have learned the art of avoiding messy people and predicaments. After all, Mary Magdalenes can really complicate a nice community.

Regardless of where you find yourself, here are a few pointers:

1. **Understand the power of patient prayer.** Too often we feel like change needs to happen right now, and in our haste we destroy the picture God has been trying to paint

in our community. Begin any effort for reform by focusing on prayer and fasting and waiting on God to move.

2. **Resist forming cliques of like-minded people within a church.** It is so easy to gradually communicate only with those who agree with us. Determine to reach out to the brothers, sisters, or families who see things a little differently. After all, the beauty of church is not the ability to pull together people who already share the same opinions. Rather it is to show how the love of Jesus can blend the lives of people with different backgrounds, financial standings, and perspectives.

3. **Be the vision you want to see in others.** Live out your ideals. If you are going to call your local church to higher ground, be sure you are modeling what you desire. Do you long for a community that lovingly submits to each other? Then be sure you are cheerfully submitting to your leadership. Do you desire a church that is actively reaching out? Then take every opportunity to reach out. Don't wait till you find the right church to start building relationships. Do it now!

4. **Don't lose sight of God's desire for close church communities.** As our communities move closer together and choose to love sacrificially, outsiders will notice and be drawn in. This is God's ultimate design for our church communities.

Church isn't always easy, and sometimes God's will for our lives isn't immediately clear. But God still desires church communities that are bound together with an obvious love for each other and a strong desire to reach out to a dying world. Following Jesus may not look the same in every culture and context, but keep God's vision before you.

CHAPTER TWENTY-SIX

Honesty About Who We Are

The early 1800s was a time of great social upheaval in England. William Wilberforce was leading the fight against slavery. Many people were moving from the countryside to inner-city London, and its crime-ridden slums were overpopulated and miserable. George Williams, still a young man when Wilberforce finally won the battle against slavery in England, saw the desperate conditions in London and was filled with compassion. George had lived a rough, sinful life as a young man, but he was converted in 1837.

George's heart went out to the many young men roaming the London streets. Many were unemployed, lived meaningless lives, and eventually became involved in crime. George began to meet with groups of these young men. He studied the Bible with them and tried to help them build a foundation on the Lord Jesus. This was a blessing to these youth, and the work grew. Other mentors were recruited, and by 1844 the society had grown to the point that George felt more structure was needed. So on June 6, 1844, an organization was officially formed and registered as the Young Men's Christian Association. We have come to know it as the YMCA.

George's original purpose was clear. This organization was to be built on the Lord Jesus Himself. George's motto for the YMCA was taken directly from Jesus' prayer as He left His disciples: "That they all may be one; as thou, Father, art in me, and I in thee, that they also may be one in us: that the world may believe that thou hast sent me."[a] George had a burning desire to improve the spiritual condition of these young men's lives.

George died in 1905, and in the years since, the YMCA has continued to grow. However, it has moved away from its original purpose, becoming known not for promoting the teachings of Jesus, but for exercise equipment, secular social programs, and indoor urban sports facilities. It has undergone a total shift in vision.

On July 12, 2010, the organization determined it was time for change. After two years of studies, they concluded that their name no longer represented them, and they began a transition. It was decided that, when referring to the larger organization, they would refer to themselves as the "Y" rather than the YMCA.[1] There were some who cried out and tried to call the organization back to its original roots. John Murray, contributor for the *Wall Street Journal,* wrote an article titled "The 'C' should stay in the YMCA," but most people took little notice. After all, why call it a Christian organization if Christian ministry hasn't

---

[a] John 17:21

been its focus for many years? The YMCA was simply being honest about who it really is.

Church: Early Vision

Have you ever wondered why the New Testament epistles to the churches say so little about reaching out? Why aren't there a few chapters outlining the best techniques to hold revivals or attract seekers, or even an outline telling the best way to bring the sinner to Christ? God plainly wants His people to reach out to the lost, so why is there so little teaching on this topic?

Interacting with people in places where Christianity is quite new, I have come to this conclusion: you don't have to tell first-generation believers to share what they have found. It happens automatically. These people know they were lost, know they had no hope, and know they have found something they want their neighbors to enjoy as well. Even if they don't tell anyone, their lives, countenances, and manner of doing business have changed so dramatically that people can't help but take note.

Evangelism in the early church was not a program or something they occasionally did. It was part of who they were. When we get a glimpse of the great love of Jesus Christ, understand His purpose and love for humanity, and grasp His vision for His church, something will happen. We won't need to have a revival once a year to reach out to the lost. It will naturally occur all year long.

Symptoms of Lost Vision

What happens when that original burden for others is lost? What happens when the Gospel becomes something primarily for the good of my family and the other families who were raised in my church? What happens when my church becomes more of a care center for residents than a hospital for hurting people? The answers to these questions may be painful, but let me share what I have observed and what I believe you will find.

You will find men who are pouring their energy into something other than the kingdom of God. You will find dairymen who cheerfully stay up all night to nurse a sick cow back to health, but who view staying up all night praying with a sin-sick struggler too much to ask. You will find men buying more land, building bigger businesses, and finding more fulfillment in profit and loss statements than in the redemption of their neighbors. You will find people who have become used to the trappings of wealth, people who profess to be following the poor Nazarene yet love exotic vacations and luxurious homes. You will find people who know all the best dining facilities in town, yet seem to have little interest in the off-scouring of society who were attracted to Jesus.

When vision is lost, you will still find the pastor proclaiming that his church is a lighthouse to the world. He will publicly acknowledge that the purpose of the church is to reach out to unbelievers. After all, this is what a Christian pastor is supposed to say. But in reality, the vast majority of his congregation has been raised inside this Christian culture. If a tattooed, sin-shattered soul ever got up enough courage to venture into the building, the people inside would struggle to know how to relate. This is what happens when vision is lost. The pastor may be a good and godly man, but when we expect no visitors in our church services, something is wrong.

> "When we expect no visitors in our church services, something is wrong."

Honesty with Who We Are

As I read about the YMCA changing its name, I have mixed feelings. Their purpose has shifted to focus almost exclusively on physical health, and that saddens me. Yet I also see something very refreshing: they are being honest about who they are. If you are going to remove Christ from the program, you should remove the "C."

I wonder if the same is true in our churches. Jesus came "to seek and to save that which was lost."[b] That was His purpose. So is it right to continue calling myself a follower of Jesus when I have little regard for the down and out? Am I rightly called a Christian if I can drive right past the people in my neighborhood and have little feeling toward their plight? And if my fellowship has become a place primarily to raise nice children and produce more good families, should we consider renaming it? Instead of calling it the Church of Jesus Christ, would it be more honest to call it the Society for Biblical Childhood Development?

A church should be a place where children are taught, nurtured, and protected, but it should not stop there. My concern should be deep not only for my children, but also for my neighbor's. As one writer has said, "Biblically, a church that fails to look at the world around it is no church at all."[2] God intends that we share what we have been given.

When I was around ten years old, Dennis started visiting our home. Dennis had been baptized as an infant into a Methodist church, raised as a nominal Presbyterian, and then decided to be baptized as a Catholic around age sixteen. After spending four years in the Marine Corps and graduating from college, Dennis had gradually distanced himself from his Catholic tradition and had become an agnostic. He felt there was probably some kind of divine source but wasn't sure what it was.

As a young boy I overheard many discussions between my father and Dennis. He was in his thirties, had a couple of children, and was struggling to know what to do with God. The time finally came when Dennis became convicted by the Lord. He confessed his faith in Jesus, repented of past sin, asked for baptism, and became part of our fellowship. Over the years since, Dennis has remained faithful to his Lord.

---

[b] Luke 19:10

I recently asked Dennis about his early life, his conversion, and his desire to join our church. What had prompted him to make such a radical change in his life? I had always suspected that his theological discussions with my father and others had been instrumental, so his answer surprised me. Dennis said the primary attraction was seeing how our families lived life together. He saw a group of people who were far from perfect, yet were trying to follow Jesus in their daily lives. I was fascinated that theology, something I thought would have been primary to this college-educated man, was not the attraction at all. I learned that raising godly children and reaching out to a lost world are not mutually exclusive visions.

> Raising godly children and reaching out to a lost world are not mutually exclusive visions.

Value of Lived Life

Too often we undervalue the impact of strong families in evangelism. We think of vibrant families as necessary to preserve the church, and evangelistic programs as necessary for expansion. But for Dennis (and he's not alone) it was vibrant families and structured lives that drew him. He saw children singing in the home, parents interacting with their families, and fathers providing good leadership. He also experienced something else—people reaching out to him in love.

Even though Dennis was educated, he had some rough edges. I can still remember staring at the tattoo on his arm and discovering that he smoked. He was just a visitor then, and I a young man, and I knew he did not fit in. Yet I was blessed to hear my parents pray for him, looking past the externals and caring about his soul and the eternal welfare of his family. Unfortunately, there are many Dennises out there who have seen nice families but have not felt accepted. I have talked to individuals who would love to experience the family stability they observe, but they never enter a church because they are not sure they would be welcome. Sadly, I am afraid some of them might not be. If we are going to reach out, we will need to love people deeply. If each follower of Jesus would simply reach out in love to his neighbor, the results could be tremendous!

Power of Multiplication

Our God loves multiplication. You can see it in nature in the law of harvest, and it was central to one of God's first commands.[c] Yet sometimes we forget the power of basic multiplication in evangelism. Recently I heard a speaker at a seminar demonstrate the power of multiplication.[3] There were almost a thousand people present, and the speaker asked everyone to assume that every person in the audience, except one, was lost. This one believer was going to focus on bringing three people in the audience to Christ in one year. So he had one person stand and select three others in the audience. Then each of these three were to find three more people and have them stand. Using this process, assuming every converted believer brought three people to the Lord, in just five years there would be 1,020 believers. Assuming this process could continue to be replicated, in sixteen years all seven billion people on the earth would be believers.

Of course, this is an incomplete picture and assumes everyone who is told believes. But before you pitch the concept, understand that it was Jesus' method. He focused on just a few men, poured time into them, walked with them, and showed them how to live. Then, just before leaving, He said, "Go ye therefore, and teach all nations, baptizing them in the name of the Father, and of the Son, and of the Holy Ghost: teaching them to observe all things whatsoever I have commanded you: and, lo, I am with you alway, even unto the end of the world."[d]

Other versions render this, "Go and make disciples of all nations."

---

[c] Genesis 1:22
[d] Matthew 28:19, 20

Go and make more followers of Jesus, plant more churches, and teach them to keep doing the same thing. Paul continued this theme when he told Timothy, "And the things that thou hast heard of me among many witnesses, the same commit thou to faithful men, who shall be able to teach others also."[e] The church at large has lost sight of this basic principle. We have focused on big meetings, big events, and big programs, yet neglected the great power and potential of simply reaching out to the person next door.

Bringing It Home
As you consider your own congregation, are you being honest about your purpose and who you really are? Are you actively involved in the lives of your neighbors? Who is sitting in your pews? It is possible to gradually morph into a Christian social club where the only ones who could ever understand all your peculiarities are those who grow up in your setting.

We won't do church perfectly, and even if we did, not everyone in our neighborhoods would be converted. Each person must make a choice, and Jesus Himself had people walk away from Him. But the important question is not really whether you are highly successful in winning outside converts. No, the question is simpler, and it is this: *Do you care?*

A follower of Jesus will care about the things He cares about and do the things He would be doing if He lived where you live. In all of our busyness it is easy to gradually lose sight of His purpose and goals. But please be honest: don't call yourself a follower of Jesus if you aren't following Him.

> Don't call yourself a follower of Jesus if you aren't following Him.

---

[e] 2 Timothy 2:2

CHAPTER TWENTY-SEVEN

A Path Forward

Throughout this book I have asked many questions with the goal of encouraging our churches to examine their vision and purpose. I believe each congregation should seriously consider whether their vision lines up with God's, and sometimes questions can help reveal that. But in this last chapter I want to go a little further and propose some steps churches can take to examine their purpose and rekindle God's vision. Jesus has assured us that His church will endure,[a] and we should take consolation from this promise. He has not assured us, however, that each congregation will survive Satan's final onslaught. Therefore it is essential that each local church take a close look at its path and purpose.

Since the day of Pentecost when the Spirit was poured out, the church has been in conflict. Satan has used both persecution and prosperity to overthrow the truth. He has worked within using false doctrine and internal conflict, while applying various forms of pressure from without. This kind of spiritual warfare has been normal.

---

[a] Matthew 16:18

But there have also been times of unusually intense spiritual battle, times when the fight for truth has been almost overwhelming and onlookers must have wondered if the true church would even survive. In these times God has called His people to rise with fervency to the battle.

Times of More

These have been times of *more*—more spiritual attack, more temptation to capitulate, more spiritual deception. This in turn has called for more from God's people: more passion for the kingdom of God, more love and commitment within churches, and more calls for collective prayer and fasting. These special times in history have required men of God to sacrifice greatly, to give up their personal ambitions, their wealth and possessions, and even their own lives for the cause of His kingdom. Increased hostility calls for increased focus on the battle, and I believe we are entering another of these times.

The Apostle Paul told Timothy, "This know also, that in the last days perilous times shall come. For men shall be lovers of their own selves, covetous, boasters, proud, blasphemers, disobedient to parents, unthankful, unholy, without natural affection, trucebreakers, false accusers, incontinent, fierce, despisers of those that are good, traitors, heady, highminded, lovers of pleasures more than lovers of God."[b]

Though this is an accurate description of our culture, Paul warns later in this chapter that this final deception will keep getting worse. "But evil men and seducers shall wax worse and worse, deceiving, and being deceived."[c] As the end of time approaches, the battle will continue to escalate in intensity. So how should we prepare? What should we be doing? Let's look at some urgent needs we have.

1. **Churches that care enough to wrestle with and write down their vision.** Habakkuk lived in a difficult time.

---

[b] 2 Timothy 3:1–4
[c] 2 Timothy 3:13

Babylon was becoming a dominant world power, and evil seemed to be winning. In his writings we see a man who was troubled and unsure at times whether God was in control. All of us can feel this way. We look around at the Christian landscape and see so much chaos in professing Christianity. Is God really going to win in the end? But notice the instruction that God gave Habakkuk: "The Lord answered me, and said, Write the vision, and make it plain upon tables, that he may run that readeth it."[d]

Businesses have known the power in vision and mission statements for years, and I believe our churches have neglected something of importance. Take time to discuss your purpose as a community of believers and write out the goals for your congregation. One congregation cannot do everything, but think about what God might be calling your church to do.

2. **Pastors willing to take risks.** If you are a leader in a church that is trying to hold a Biblical line against the constant pressure from our Western culture, you are already extremely busy! You are being pulled in many different directions, and a good week is seven days without a major crisis in your congregation. You, of all people in your congregation, are well aware of fault lines within your church. You have muscle pulling one way and bone another, and you may fear that open discussion might prove catastrophic. I plead with you to rethink this position.

There is a time for carefully structured meetings, but it is also important to hear what God is saying through the body. Muscle and bone in the church will never work in a coordinated way until they understand the blessing

---

[d] Habakkuk 2:2

and purpose the other brings to the body of Christ, and this will only be accomplished by closer relationship. Ignoring differences will seldom make them go away, but communicating in love can cause a church to begin functioning as God intended. We need more pastors who are willing to take the risk of open dialogue.

3. **Energetic young warriors who are willing to wait.** There is also a great need for youth who are willing to patiently follow. One of the reasons older leaders are afraid to take risks is because they are unsure how committed their reformers are. Youth who see apathy within a fellowship need to speak up, but they need to do so privately and respectfully, assuring their leaders of their commitment to their local brotherhood. They also need to be aware that there are good reasons for not making changes too quickly. Reformers are not typically patient, but if a church is going to demonstrate the kingdom of God to a lost world, time must be given for change. A man with the gift of prophecy usually calls for instant reform. The issues are black and white, and if change is needed, why delay? But the man with the gift of pastoring has a deep concern for those on the fringes. He is afraid that the weak will be lost if reform occurs too rapidly.

The church has a great need for both prophets and pastors. We need prophets among us who can identify the problems, men like the "children of Issachar, which were men that had understanding of the times, to know what Israel ought to do."[e] But they need to understand that changing minds takes time, and that some of their ideas may not be correct. They may need to be honed by older believers with more experience. The church today needs patient prophets.

---

[e] 1 Chronicles 12:32

4. **Churches with a purpose beyond themselves.** Should every decision be based on what is best for us, every pursuit have a goal of enhancing our own lives, and every activity be focused on improving our church or school? Many of these things are good and important, but when we become so focused on ourselves that we are too busy to build a relationship with the neighbor across the road, something is dreadfully wrong. There is a great need for churches with a local vision and purpose. It isn't hard to raise money to send off to the other side of the globe—and it is important to do this—but we also need churches willing to demonstrate the kingdom of God locally.

5. **Older believers who lead by example.** We desperately need older believers who are willing to spend the last twenty years of their lives actively living for the kingdom. There are few things that encourage youth like seeing older warriors still willing to engage in the battle. Years ago I talked to a brother in his eighties who was still extremely active. He had cancer, but rather than pursing all the health options out there, he was using every day to reach out to others. He told me, "I don't have much time left, but I want to use every day God gives me to share what I have been given!"

I listened as he shared some of his experiences working with inner-city people, and I left that discussion inspired. Here was a man who really believed in the kingdom of God, and his last years were a demonstration of that fact. But I wondered why there weren't more believers like this, more older people willing to work with dysfunctional families, troubled marriages, and disoriented youth. Why weren't more people walking away from successful business, moving out into new areas, and planting more churches? Our churches need more people who, in their older years, embrace the exciting vocation of being coworkers with God as He continues to expand His kingdom!

6. **Churches that unashamedly pursue a counterculture path.** True seekers are not drawn to someone who looks, talks, and acts like the world. When God draws a man, He calls him to conform himself to Jesus Christ, and this automatically puts him on a counterculture path. Consequently, he will be searching for people who are traveling on a similar trajectory. He will identify with those who have seen the emptiness of temporal pursuits and have cheerfully chosen to follow our Lord. As followers of Jesus, we should never be ashamed of being different from the world. Rather, we should be embarrassed when we aren't.

> We should never be ashamed of being different from the world. Rather, we should be embarrassed when we aren't.

7. **Churches capable of developing close relationships.** We are not capable of maintaining close connections with a large number of people. While Jesus had compassion on the multitudes and reached out to large crowds, His inner circle was quite small. If our churches are going to successfully hold each other accountable, demonstrate self-sacrificing love to the lost, and enjoy the blessing of leaders who have the time to reach out, we will need to prayerfully consider the size of our congregations. When each member is needed and utilized, a congregation will be much more apt to enjoy the blessings God intended.

Small congregations tend to have less potential for pride within leadership, less burnout, and more opportunity for close relationships.

The larger a church is, the more its administrative machinery will begin to feel like a business, as it must expend more energy to preserve itself. And with more activity going on internally, there will be less energy to expend on the strugglers and seekers without. This does not mean that smaller is always better. There are plenty of stories out there of disunited small congregations. But I have observed that harmonious music tends to come from small groups of closely knit believers—churches that operate more like a family and less like a business. When churches grow beyond the capability of making decisions through close relationship, something vital is lost.

8. **Church families rather than family churches.** There is a great difference between a church family and a church that is simply a gathering of families. In a family church, the congregation's function is to serve the families within. In a church family, the members serve the church. In a family church, the biological family unit is preeminent. Consequently, the older single or the seeker who desires to join but is not part of a strong biological family will always feel somewhat disconnected. When families gather during certain holidays, the single mother from the community will feel disconnected. The fact that she is different will become evident as she discovers that the biological family means more in the congregation than the church family.

In a church family where the community becomes the dominant relationship, a congregation becomes a welcome place for those who feel rejected by society. For this to occur, the traditions of the church family must become stronger and contain a richness and importance that supersedes the biological family. They may include special yearly events, specific cultural customs, or even ways the church has agreed to dress. This area needs to be analyzed frequently since it is easy for traditions to become more important than Biblical principle. Yet when kept within their proper place, rich church family traditions can help seekers integrate into the church and assist them in feeling like family.

Church: The Tremendous Potential
We greatly underestimate the incredible possibilities in our church communities. It is no wonder the early church grew. They were family! Even in the middle of heavy persecution, being chased by lions and burned at the stake, beautiful music was coming forth. They had a strong love for each other and for their Lord. They were excited about their message, their goal being to share this new song with as many as would listen. But is this still possible today? Could God, in these last days, again inspire His church and empower it to produce that same compelling music that soared from those first believers? They weren't perfect; they had some major issues and produced some discordant notes. But those who experienced the initial beauty of believers working harmoniously never forgot the beauty of that song. The apostles wrote the epistles, calling churches to focus on their Lord, love each other, and get back to the task of singing on key.

Picture churches today, small groups of people scattered around the globe, so dedicated to following Jesus and loving each other that their own personal preferences are forgotten. Imagine congregations focused on the conductor, Jesus Himself, rather than on each other. Allow your mind to hear beautiful music floating out of the windows of churches like that. Visualize congregations committed to that early vision of the Gospel spreading by multiplication—not a vision of building local empires, but spreading out, planting more churches, providing new music in new places. Evangelist Luis Palau once said, "The church is like manure. Pile it together and it stinks up the neighborhood; spread it out and it enriches the world."[1]

Continued church planting is the obvious precedent set by the early disciples. We see them quickly moving out over the known world, and I believe every healthy church should be considering and praying about planting new churches. This is the pattern we see in Acts, and it is still God's will today.

Follow Me

Jesus' message to His disciples was simple. "If any man will come after me, let him deny himself, and take up his cross, and follow me."[f] Though not a complicated message, it cut across their personal desires. When each of us individually launches out in faith, trusts in His strength, and intentionally puts His teachings into action, a beautiful collective song will emerge.

So start today. Invite people over who have no way to repay. Start loving that difficult brother in your congregation and treat him as you would like to be treated. Find ways to befriend the lonely and downcast in your local town. Visit a rest home and take time to read or pray with a few residents. Reach out to that coworker who has trouble maintaining relationships. Stop avoiding that difficult sister and love her as you would like to be loved. The list could go on. There is no shortage of places where the song of God's kingdom needs to be sung. As you sing the part God has given you, have confidence that others will join in, and His music will begin to impact your community.

God has called us to live out His song, not just for our own good, but for the good of His kingdom and to the praise of His glory. May the Lord bless you and your church as you produce His music. May His song be sung through you!

---

[f] Matthew 16:24

ENDNOTES

CHAPTER ONE
1 Rebecca Rupp, <http://theplate.nationalgeographic.com/2014/08/13/the-butter-wars-when-margarine-was-pink/>, accessed on 3/20/17.
2 Rory Sutherland, <http://www.campaignlive.com/article/tips-marlboro-man/1214274>, accessed on 3/21/17.
3 Malcolm Gladwell, *Blink,* Back Bay Books, New York, 2005, p. 160.
4 Rick Warren, <http://pastors.com/preach-like-jesus-1/>, accessed on 3/27/17.

CHAPTER THREE
1 <http://www.bodyworlds.com/en.html>, accessed on 8/11/16.

CHAPTER FOUR
1 Mark Martin, <http://www1.cbn.com/cbnnews/us/2011/December/Handels-Messiah-Inspires-Listeners-Transcends-Time>, accessed on 4/7/17.
2 <http://www.christianity.com/church/church-history/timeline/1701-1800/messiah-and-george-frideric-handel-11630237.html?_sm_au_=iHVM7FZwpQs6R6sH>, accessed on 8/9/16.

CHAPTER FIVE
1 A.W. Tozer, *That Incredible Christian,* Tyndale House Publishers, Wheaton, Illinois, 1964, p. 92.
2 <https://www.brainyquote.com/quotes/leo_tolstoy_105644>, accessed on 2/20/18.

CHAPTER SEVEN
1 Chris Wild, <http://mashable.com/2015/05/27/swimsuit-police/#39ioed6Ggkqm>, accessed on 8/31/16.
2 Lewis Loflin, <http://www.sullivan-county.com/news/>, accessed on 9/1/16.
3 Ben Quinn, <https://www.theguardian.com/world/2016/aug/24/french-police-make-woman-remove-burkini-on-nice-beach>, accessed on 9/1/16.

CHAPTER NINE
1 Rod Dreher, *The Benedict Option,* Penguin Random House, New York, 2017, p. 121.
2 Roland H. Bainton, "The Enduring Witness," *Mennonite Life,* April 1954.
3 John Coblentz, *Are Written Standards for the Church?* Christian Light Publications, Harrisonburg, Virginia, 1990, p.14.
4 Joel Richardson, <https://books.google.com/books?id=_lyXZu3d3OcC&pg=PA26&lpg=PA26&dq=american+inner+cities+conversion+Islam&source=bl&ots=HPArPVCQWE&sig=wJVuhxvL_10kReL9zKomubetbwM&hl=en&sa=X&ved=0ahUKEwjx5tfw7ubXAhUE42MKHRzYAuoQ6AEIXzAJ#v=onepage&q=american%20inner%20cities%20conversion%20Islam&f=false>, accessed on 2/9/18.

CHAPTER ELEVEN
[1] Thieleman J. Braght, *Martyrs Mirror,* 5th ed., Herald Press, Scottdale, Pennsylvania, 1950, pp. 8–10.
[2] Ibid., p. 10.
[3] George Orwell, *Animal Farm: A Fairy Story,* Harcourt, Brace, and Company, New York, 1946.

CHAPTER SIXTEEN
[1] The Octavius of Minucius Felix, *Ante-Nicene Fathers,* Volume IV, Chap. XXXVIII, Eerdmans Publishing Company, Edinburgh, 1989, p. 197.

CHAPTER SEVENTEEN
[1] Alan Wolk, <https://www.theguardian.com/media-network/2015/jun/22/30-second-commercial-advertising-outdated>, accessed on 1/9/17.
[2] Frank Newport, <http://www.gallup.com/poll/187955/percentage-christians-drifting-down-high.aspx>, accessed on 1/6/17.
[3] Dalia Sussman, <http://abcnews.go.com/US/Beliefs/story?id=1422658>, accessed on 1/6/17.
[4] N.T. Wright, *Simply Jesus,* Harper Collins, New York, 2011, p. 218.

CHAPTER EIGHTEEN
[1] Real Time with Bill Maher, <http://www.hbo.com/real-time-with-bill-maher/episodes/0/213-episode/video/clip-new-rule-thy-will-be-gun.html?autoplay=true>, accessed on 1/11/17.

CHAPTER TWENTY
[1] Roy B. Zuck, *The Speaker's QuoteBook,* Kregal Publications, Grand Rapids, Michigan, 1997, p. 108.
[2] Finny Kurvilla, *King Jesus Claims His Church,* Anchor Cross Publishing, Cambridge, Massachusetts, 2013, p. X.

CHAPTER TWENTY-ONE
[1] Gretchen Livingston, <http://www.pewresearch.org/fact-tank/2014/12/22/less-than-half-of-u-s-kids-today-live-in-a-traditional-family/>, accessed on 1/17/17.
[2] Ed Stetzer, <http://www.christianitytoday.com/edstetzer/2014/february/marriage-divorce-and-body-of-christ-what-do-stats-say-and-c.html>, accessed on 1/17/17.

CHAPTER TWENTY-TWO
[1] Val Yoder, *I Will Build My Church,* Kitchi Blessings Ministries, Blackduck, Minnesota, 2000, p. 126.

CHAPTER TWENTY-THREE
[1] Michael J. Miller, <http://forwardthinking.pcmag.com/software/286148-the-rise-of-dos-how-microsoft-got-the-ibm-pc-os-contract>, and Michael Laws, <http://www.computerhistory.org/atchm/gary-kildall-40th-anniversary-of-the-birth-of-the-pc-operating-system/>, both accessed on 1/23/17. We may never know all the facts. Gary Kildall argued years later that he had traveled to an important business meeting, while Bill Gates said that "Gary was out flying." But whatever the exact reason for the flight, Gary Kildall would obviously have stayed at the office if he could have known the future.

CHAPTER TWENTY-FOUR
[1] Brother Yun, *Living Water,* Zondervan, Grand Rapids, Michigan, 2008, p. 170.

CHAPTER TWENTY-FIVE
[1] Rod Dreher, *The Benedict Option,* Penguin Random House, New York, 2017, p. 96.
[2] *The Economist,* "Deaths of Despair," Vol. 442, Num. 9033, March 25–31, 2017, p. 67.
[3] Dietrich Bonhoeffer, *Life Together,* Harper Collins Publishers, New York, 1954, p. 27.

CHAPTER TWENTY-SIX
[1] <http://www.ymca.net/news-releases/news-releases-20100712-brand-new-day.html>, accessed on 1/30/17.
[2] Francis Chan, *Multiply: Disciples Making Disciples,* David Cook Distribution, Colorado Springs, Colorado, 2012, p. 66.
[3] Finny Kurvilla, "Multiplication and Discipleship," <https://kingdomfellowshipweekend.org/audio>, accessed on 1/30/17.

CHAPTER TWENTY-SEVEN
[1] Philip Yancey, *Church: Why Bother?,* Zondervan Publishing, Grand Rapids, Michigan, 1998, p. 33.

About the Author

Gary Miller was raised in California and today lives with his wife Patty and family in the Pacific Northwest. Gary works with the poor in developing countries and directs the SALT Microfinance Solutions program for Christian Aid Ministries. This program offers business and spiritual teaching to those living in chronic poverty, provides small loans, sets up local village savings groups, and assists them in learning how to use their God-given resources to become sustainable.

Gary has authored the Kingdom-Focused Living Series, microfinance manuals, and several booklets for outreach purposes. For a list of his books and other resource materials, see page 239.

Have you been inspired by Gary's materials? Maybe you have questions, or perhaps you even disagree with the author. Share your thoughts by sending an e-mail to kingdomfinance@camoh.org or writing to Christian Aid Ministries, P.O. Box 360, Berlin, Ohio 44610.

Additional Resources by Gary Miller

BOOKS

Kingdom-Focused Finances for the Family
This first book in the Kingdom-Focused Living series is realistic, humorous, and serious about getting us to become stewards instead of owners.

Charting a Course in Your Youth
A serious call to youth to examine their faith, focus, and finances. Second book in Kingdom-Focused Living series.

Going Till You're Gone
A plea for godly examples—for older men and women who will demonstrate a kingdom-focused vision all the way to the finish line. Third book in Kingdom-Focused Living series.

The Other Side of the Wall
Stresses Biblical principles that apply to all Christians who want to reflect God's heart in giving. Applying these principles has the potential to change lives—first our own, and then the people God calls us to share with. Fourth book in Kingdom-Focused Living series.

It's Not Your Business
How involved in business should followers of Jesus be? Did God intend the workplace to play a prominent role in building his kingdom? Explore the benefits and dangers in business. Fifth and final book in the Kingdom-Focused Living series.

Budgeting Made Simple
A budgeting workbook in a ring binder; complements *Kingdom-Focused Finances for the Family*.

What Happened to Our Money?
Ignorance of Biblical money management can set young people on a path of financial hardship that results in anxiety, marital discord, depression, and envy. This short book presents foundational truths on which young couples can build their financial lives.

Life in a Global Village
Would your worldview change if the world population were shrunk to a village of one hundred people and you lived in that village? Full-color book.

This Side of the Global Wall
Pictures and graphs in this full-color book portray the unprecedented opportunities Americans have today. What are we doing with the resources God has given us?

Small Business Handbook
A manual used in microfinance programs in developing countries. Includes devotionals and practical business teaching. Ideal for missions and churches.

Following Jesus in Everyday Life
A teaching manual ideal for mission settings. Each lesson addresses a Biblical principle and includes a story and discussion questions. Black and white illustrations.

A Good Soldier of Jesus Christ

A teaching manual like *Following Jesus in Everyday Life*, but targeting youth.

Know Before You Go

Every year, thousands of Americans travel to distant countries to help the needy. But could some of these short-term mission trips be doing more harm than good? This book encourages us to reexamine our goals and methods, and prepares people to effectively interact with other cultures in short-term missions.

Jesus Really Said That?

This book presents five teachings of Jesus that are often missed, ignored, or rejected. It tells the story of Jeremy and Alicia, a couple who thought they understood Christianity and knew what it meant to be a Christian . . . until they began to look at what Jesus actually said!

Radical Islam

From the barbarous actions of ISIS to the shocking tactics of Al-Qaida, radical Islamic extremists seem to be everywhere and growing stronger. Many wonder in alarm if the movement will overtake the West and change Americans' way of life forever. How should Christians respond to this threat? Does the Bible have answers? How would Jesus respond?

How Can Anyone Say God Is Good?

Nick is fed up with life and aggravated by the simple-minded people who believe in a supreme being in spite of all the agony and chaos around them. How can they have the audacity to say their God is good? Written in story form and ending with the author's personal journey, this book is a good gift for an agnostic or atheist friend. It can also be used to strengthen the faith of a Christian believer.

AUDIO BOOKS

Kingdom-Focused Finances for the Family
Charting a Course in Your Youth
Going Till You're Gone
The Other Side of the Wall
It's Not Your Business
Life in a Global Village

SEMINARS

Kingdom-Focused Finances—Audio
This three-session seminar takes you beyond our culture's view of money and possessions, and challenges you to examine your heart by looking at your treasure. Three CDs.

Kingdom-Focused Finances—Audio and Visual
Follow along on the slides Gary uses in his seminars while you listen to the presentation. A good tool for group study or individual use. A computer is needed to view these three CDs.

About Christian Aid Ministries

Christian Aid Ministries was founded in 1981 as a nonprofit, tax-exempt 501(c)(3) organization. Its primary purpose is to provide a trustworthy and efficient channel for Amish, Mennonite, and other conservative Anabaptist groups and individuals to minister to physical and spiritual needs around the world. This is in response to the command to ". . . do good unto all men, especially unto them who are of the household of faith" (Galatians 6:10).

Each year, CAM supporters provide 15-20 million pounds of food, clothing, medicines, seeds, Bibles, Bible story books, and other Christian literature for needy people. Most of the aid goes to orphans and Christian families. Supporters' funds also help to clean up and rebuild for natural disaster victims, put up Gospel billboards in the U.S., support several church-planting efforts, operate two medical clinics, and provide resources for needy families to make their own living. CAM's main purposes for providing aid are to help and encourage God's people and bring the Gospel to a lost and dying world.

CAM has staff, warehouses, and distribution networks in

Romania, Moldova, Ukraine, Haiti, Nicaragua, Liberia, Israel, and Kenya. Aside from management, supervisory personnel, and bookkeeping operations, volunteers do most of the work at CAM locations. Each year, volunteers at our warehouses, field bases, Disaster Response Services projects, and other locations donate over 200,000 hours of work.

CAM's ultimate purpose is to glorify God and help enlarge His kingdom. ". . . whatsoever ye do, do all to the glory of God" (1 Corinthians 10:31).

The Way to God and Peace

We live in a world contaminated by sin. Sin is anything that goes against God's holy standards. When we do not follow the guidelines that God our Creator gave us, we are guilty of sin. Sin separates us from God, the source of life.

Since the time when the first man and woman, Adam and Eve, sinned in the Garden of Eden, sin has been universal. The Bible says that we all have "sinned and come short of the glory of God" (Romans 3:23). It also says that the natural consequence for that sin is eternal death, or punishment in an eternal hell: "Then when lust hath conceived, it bringeth forth sin: and sin, when it is finished, bringeth forth death" (James 1:15).

But we do not have to suffer eternal death in hell. God provided a sacrifice for our sins through the gift of His only Son, Jesus Christ. "For God so loved the world that he gave his only begotten Son, that whosoever believeth in him should not perish, but have everlasting life" (John 3:16).

A sacrifice is something given to benefit someone else. It costs the giver greatly. Jesus was God's sacrifice. Jesus' death takes away the penalty of sin for all those who accept this sacrifice and truly repent of their sins. To repent of sins means to be truly sorry for and turn away from the things we have done that have violated God's standards (Acts 2:38; 3:19).

Jesus died, but He did not remain dead. After three days, God's Spirit miraculously raised Him to life again. God's Spirit does something similar in us. When we receive Jesus as our sacrifice and repent of our sins, our hearts are changed. We become spiritually alive! We develop new desires and attitudes (2 Corinthians 5:17). We begin to make choices that please God (1 John 3:9). If we do fail and commit sins, we can ask God for forgiveness. "If we confess our sins, he is faithful and just to forgive us our sins, and to cleanse us from all unrighteousness" (1 John 1:9).

Once our hearts have been changed, we want to continue growing spiritually. We will be happy to let Jesus be the Master of our lives and will want to become more like Him. To do this, we must meditate on God's Word and commune with God in prayer. We will testify to others of this change by being baptized and sharing the good news of God's victory over sin and death. Fellowship with a faithful group of believers will strengthen our walk with God (1 John 1:7).